Inhalt

Ulrich Klinge / Volker Möbius

TRAINING
Working with Texts

Basic Skills / Sekundarstufe II

Beilage: Lösungsheft

Ernst Klett Verlag für Wissen und Bildung
Stuttgart · Dresden

Zeichnung auf Seite 81: K. Brückmann, Stuttgart

Die Deutsche Bibliothek – CIP-Einheitsaufnahme

Klinge, Ulrich:
Training Working with Texts: Basic Skills, Sekundarstufe II/
von Ulrich Klinge und Volker Möbius. – 1.Aufl. –
Stuttgart; Dresden: Klett, Verlag für Wissen und Bildung, 1994
ISBN 3-12-922114-X

 Gedruckt auf Papier, das aus chlorfrei
gebleichtem Zellstoff hergestellt wurde.

1. Auflage 1994
Alle Rechte vorbehalten
Fotomechanische Wiedergabe nur mit Genehmigung des Verlages.
© Ernst Klett Verlag für Wissen und Bildung GmbH, Stuttgart 1994
Druck: W. Röck, Weinsberg
Einband- und Innengestaltung: Hitz und Mahn, Stuttgart
ISBN 3-12-922114-X

Einleitung

Aktuelle englische Zeitungsartikel verstehen, Werbetexte analysieren, Meinungs-kommentare in Aufbau und Aussage erfassen, englischsprachige Literaturaus-schnitte verschiedenster Gattungen verstehen und deuten – das geschieht doch schon seit Jahren im Unterricht. Nichts Neues also? Richtig. Aber wie steht es mit der schriftlichen Textanalyse in Klausuren oder gar im Abitur? Leistet das der Englischunterricht ebenfalls?

Es ist das Ziel dieses Bandes, in elementare Kategorien der Analyse von Texten einzuführen, d.h. erlernbare Methoden der Textinterpretation einzuüben, die dafür benötigten Sach- und Gelenkvokabeln zu vermitteln und den Schüler zur schriftli-chen Ausformulierung seiner Arbeitsergebnisse anzuleiten.

Dieser Band gliedert sich in 15 Kapitel, die etwa zur Hälfte nichtfiktionale und fiktionale Texte berücksichtigen. Jedes Kapitel konzentriert sich auf einen oder zwei Analyseschwerpunkte; sie erfassen charakteristische Merkmale einer vorgestellten Textsorte. Dabei liegt das Hauptgewicht eindeutig auf dem methodischen Lernen: Wie gehe ich bei der Analyse von Texten aus der englischsprachigen Presse und Literatur im einzelnen vor? Jeder Schüler kann sich diese Methodik selbst aneignen und leicht auf weitere Texte übertragen.

Das Trainingsbuch enthält klar aufeinander aufbauende Handlungsanweisungen (Steps) und eine Fülle von sprachlichen Formulierungshilfen. Darauf abgestimmt gibt es ein Lösungsheft, in dem für die A- und B-Teile der Kapitel ausführliche Stichwort-sammlungen und komplette Aufgabenlösungen nachzulesen sind. Die Aufgaben unter Comment/Composition können frei und ohne einengende Vorgaben bearbeitet werden.

Working with Texts erlaubt sowohl einen systematischen Durchgang als auch einen direkten Zugriff auf einzelne, ausgewählte Analysekategorien. Das Inhaltsverzeichnis und Querverweise in den Kapiteln erleichtern eine rasche Orientierung. Eventuelle inhaltliche oder sprachliche Verständnisschwierigkeiten werden durch eine umfang-reiche Wortliste am Ende des Buches aufgefangen (Glossar). Die Liste enthält Übersetzungshilfen zu den Arbeitsanweisungen und Word-boxes in den einzelnen Kapiteln (Themen- und Gelenkvokabular).

Besonders danken wir unseren englischen Freunden Karen und Mike Norman aus Crawley, West Sussex, die uns wertvolle Anregungen und Tips gaben, und einigen Kolleginnen und Kollegen, die Teile des Manuskripts im Unterricht erprobten.

Troisdorf und Königswinter-Vinxel   Juni 1994

Topic: *Comprehension, Summary, Personal Opinion*   **Text 1**

U.S. Epidemic: Armed Youths
'I Put On My Shoes, My Pants, My Shirt and My Gun'
BY JOSEPH B. TREASTER AND MARY. B. W. TABOR

NEW YORK – On a shadowy corner in Brooklyn, a gangly teenager slowly opened his jacket to give a peek at the 9 mm semiautomatic pistol jammed in the waistband of his jeans. "When you've got it," he said, glancing at the weapon, "you've got the power. It doesn't matter whether you're big or small. You've got the power."

In a nearby pizza parlor, two young men said they felt naked without their guns. "It's like an article of clothing," one explained. "I put on my shoes, my pants,
5 my shirt, my hat and my gun."
Throughout the city these days, there are teenagers toting guns from the arsenal of tens of thousands of pistols and revolvers, sawed-off shotguns and submachine guns
10 that have been flooding in on the surging currents of riches and violence in the nation's biggest drug market.
New York is hardly alone. Experts say that all around the country teenagers are taking
15 up guns. "The number of young people arming themselves and dying is reaching epidemic proportions," said Vanessa Scherzer, a spokeswoman for the Center to Prevent Handgun Violence. "It's happening
20 in big cities and small towns."
Some young gunslingers are dealers, runners and neighborhood managers in the drug trade. Some are muggers who learned quickly that one glimpse of a gun was
25 enough to make most people turn over a wallet or a purse in a flash. But as guns have proliferated, many young people have been caught up in a vicious circle of packing weapons to protect themselves.
30 "You get it because you fear what is happening out there," said a New York teenager. "Once you have it you feel like a god. You feel invincible."
Certainly not every young person carries a
35 gun. "But," said Catherine M. Abate, commissioner of probation in New York City, "it's no longer the exception – it's commonplace."
"Guns and kids are probably the most
40 dangerous combination there is," said Peter Reinharz, the head of the Family Court Division of the city's Corporation Counsel who serves as New York's chief prosecutor of youths under 16. "A 13- or 14-year-old
45 holding an Uzi submachine gun has no understanding of his own mortality, let alone your mortality."

International Herald Tribune, February 2, 1992
Copyright © 1992 by The New York Times Company. Reprinted by permission.

Annotations:
gangly – belonging to a gang; give a peek at – give a quick look at; jammed in the waistband – in den Gürtel gesteckt; l.1 pizza parlor – shop selling pizza; l.7 tote guns – carry guns; l.9 sawed-off – abgesägt; l.10 surging currents – anschwellender Strom; l.21 gunslinger – Revolverheld; l.23 mugger – s.b. who robs people with a gun; l.24 glimpse – short look; l.27 proliferate – increase in number; l.28 vicious circle – Teufelskreis; l.33 invincible – unbesiegbar; l.36 commissioner of probation – Beauftragte für die Bewährung von Straffälligen; l.38 commonplace – normal; l.42 Corporation Counsel – Verbandsanwalt; l.43 chief prosecutor – Staatsanwalt.

A. Comprehension

1. What feelings do the weapon-carrying teenagers describe in the *New York Times* article? (3–4 sentences)
2. For what purposes do they use their pistols, revolvers, shotguns and such like? (2–3 sentences)
3. Why do the authors speak of an 'arsenal' (l.7), of 'flooding' (l.10) and of 'surging currents' (ll. 10/11) when describing the picture ' all around the country'? (2–3 sentences)
4. What does the use of the word 'epidemic' (title; l.17) suggest in that context? (2 sentences)
5. What does Peter Reinharz call the most dangerous combination and why does he do so? (3–4 sentences)

How to answer comprehension questions on a text

Step 1   Read through the text without interruption using any vocabulary and other helpful tips given to understand its **gist** (= Kernaussage).

Step 2   After you have grasped what the text is about (topic? problem? main point?), go through the questions making sure you understand what each of the questions is aiming at.

Step 3   Read the text again, this time looking **for detail**; use a pencil or text marker to identify relevant passages, key sentences, and important words (who? where? what?).

Example

New York — On a shadowy corner in Brooklyn, a gangly teenager slowly opened his jacket to give a peek at the 9 mm semiautomatic pistol jammed in the waistband of his jeans. 'When you've got it,' he said, glancing at the weapon, 'you've got the power. It doesn't matter whether you are big or small. You've got the power.'

As you set out to answer the comprehension questions on our text, take this advice:

Be careful
In their written answers students tend to quote or copy from the text itself. This is considered bad style by your teacher! Rather than "play it safe" (= copy from the text) you should try to use your own vocabulary. This is as important as your coming to grips with the text itself.

Step 4   Study the following model answer to question 1:

Example

In the New York Times *article three teenagers speak out on carrying a weapon. One of them says that a gun is part of his daily outfit, otherwise he would feel unprotected. Two others argue that weapons help them to overcome fear and give a feeling of strength. One even states that he feels like a god - omnipotent.*

Step 5   Note how the vocabulary of the original text has been changed.

tote guns	➡	carry guns
article of clothing	➡	part of his daily outfit
naked	➡	unprotected
feeling of power	➡	strength
feel like a god	➡	omnipotent

Step 6   Go back to part A, page 7 and answer the five questions on the text.

B. Summary Writing

Info
If you can write the **summary** of a text, you show that you have understood the essence (= the key points) of the text quite well. A **summary** is, first of all, an **objective version** of the original text. It does not suppress any facts, data or events, thus slanting the text in any way, and it does not add anything new in the way of or interpreting the text or giving a personal comment on it. But a **summary** is also a **compressed** (=shorter) **version** of the text. If you want to score with your summary, there are a few rules to be respected:

Basic rules of the summary:

> – Try to stick to what the text says; do not go for interpretation or meaning.
> – Try to avoid any personal or other comment.
> – Include important facts, aspects, events only.
> – Exclude all unimportant = expendable details.
> – Try to compress = cut down vocabulary and long sentences.
> – Avoid copying the vocabulary of the text; use your own words.
> – Do not include direct speech and text quotations.
> – A summary is preferably written in present tense (simple form).

How to write a summary

Step 1   For starters, much of what has been said in part A is true for **summary technique** as well. So if you did the comprehension questions, especially Steps 1 and 2, part of your work has been done already.

Step 2   Go over your marked (or unmarked) text again and break it down to its key elements (relevant points, key sentences, key words) and list them. This is sometimes called the 'skeleton' (= the bones) of a text.

Example

Possible list covering paragraphs 1 and 2 of text:

New York, Brooklyn
teenager
a peek at the 9 mm semiautomatic
power (2x)

two young men
feel naked without gun
an article of clothing
shoes, pants, shirt, hat, gun

Step 3   Before doing your summary, you might consider going over your 'skeleton' list again and doing a little **vocabulary exercise**.

Take down a few synonyms and vocabulary alternatives that will help you to replace the text vocabulary where necessary.
In case your memory fails you, there are excellent word-finding dictionaries around: i.e.*Chambers Thesaurus. A Comprehensive Wordfinding Dictionary*, Chambers Cambridge, Paperback Edition 1989.

Example

This is what your word list might look like:

teenager	*kid, youngster, youth*
a peek at	*a look at, revealing, displaying*
power	*strength, self-confidence*
feel naked	*feel undressed, feel unsafe*
article of clothing	*dress, outfit*
…	
…	

Step 4 Now write a summary of *U.S. Epidemic: Armed Youths* in about 120
words. Your summary might begin like this:

"In their New York Times *article J.B.Treaster and M.B.W. Tabor
report on the new wave of weapon-carrying youths in the U.S. At the
beginning they quote teenagers who profess that weapons are part
of …"*

C. Comment/Composition

1. Imagine you are an elder sister/brother of one of the teenagers mentioned in the
   article. How would you answer him to make him understand what he is doing?

2. Which of these remedies or policies to cope with teenage violence would you
   personally favour ?

Annotations:
remedies – measures to cope with the
problem
restraints – more caution, stricter limits
legally liable – responsible

REMEDIES	% who favor these actions as ways to reduce teenage violence:
Tougher criminal penalties for juvenile offenders	**79%**
More government spending on educational and recreational facilities for teenagers	**73%**
Greater restraints on the showing of sex and violence on television	**73%**
Greater restraints on the showing of sex and violence in movies	**70%**
Greater restraints on sex and violence in rock-music lyrics	**64%**
Holding parents legally liable for the violent criminal actions of their children	**46%**

From a telephone poll of 506 adult Americans taken for TIME/CNN on June 1 by Yankelovich Clancy
Shulman. Sampling error is plus or minus 4.5%.   TIME Charts by Cynthia Davis

How to write a personal comment

Info

The two tasks above invite you to **state your own opinion** on the topic of the *New York Times* article. This is called **writing a personal comment**. A comment normally combines **fact** and **opinion**. You start out from given facts or events and then express your personal judgement, leaving no doubt as to where you personally stand.

Step 1   Let us say you have made up your mind and are quite sure of what your position is. You collect your ideas and arguments in a first draft. Study the following example (question 1):

Example

- *weapons are not for little boys*

- *whoever has a weapon will use it sooner or later*

- *ever thought of possible consequences?*

- *not only harm (innocent) people, also risk your own life*

- *shooting at people is no solution; using violence calls for more violence*

- *can understand that you are frightened to go out*

- *if attacked everybody has the right to protect himself*

- *boys are expected to be tough, not to be wimps*

Step 2   Write an answer to comment question 1 in 100–120 words.

Step 3   Now let us deal with comment question 2. Read the "Remedies" (p. 10) and decide which of them you would favour.

Step 4   Collect your ideas and arguments as in Step 1.

Info

To be effective your comment must be clear and comprehensible. It must have a **clear beginning**, a **discernible middle**, an **convincing end:** it needs **structure!**

To take off forcefully, use expressions such as:

> It is often argued that …
> It is widely believed that …
> A commonly held view is that …

A forceful **beginning** is always important. Next there is the **argumentation** to be considered. To emphasize your standpoint you need effective 'phrases and expressions of opinion'.

Be careful
'I think' and 'I'm of the opinion that' sound rather lame, don't they? Keep an eye on the way English authors express their opinions and start a little collection?
Perhaps you can use some of the following:

| If you feel certain … | … unsure or |
| … or pretty sure | … doubtful |

There is no question that…	I wonder if/ why …
I am (quite) certain that …	I am doubtful whether …
I am (firmly) convinced that …	I am in two minds about …
There is no denying that …	Couldn't it be that …?
I (firmly) believe that …	I cannot really believe
	that …

To conclude your comment use phrases such as:

> All in all …
> To summarize ….
> To put it in a nutshell …

Select 4–5 expressions from the vocabulary boxes that you are going to include in your comment.

Step 5   Read this fine example of a personal comment on question 2 by 11th-grader Stephanie Bartels from Troisdorf. Mark the 'expressions of opinion' Stephanie has used and add them to your active vocabulary.

It is often argued that tougher criminal penalties would stop the rising of teenage violence. But I don't believe that kids fear the penalties for what they have done. I'm quite certain that most of the criminal teenagers think that nobody can catch them, and the others are sure that it isn't wrong to kill somebody if you don't know what to do otherwise.
And that's the point. I am firmly convinced that there must be more government spending on educational and recreational facilities. Many parents are not interested in their children or they have no time for them. Therefore the kids have to be educated by other people who care for them and their problems.
I believe that teenagers who don't know how to spend their free time hang around with their friends and then commit crimes like wilding and marauding.
And although it could be that (some other) youths try to destroy the facilities, I'm sure that this is the only solution to get the youngsters away from the street and their gangs.

Step 6   Has everything gone down well with you so far?
Now pick another one of the "remedies" from the *Time* survey and write your personal comment. It should not be too difficult!

Topic: *Comprehension and Summary of a News Story*   **Text 2**

'He just lay there and quietly slipped away. It was very peaceful. I was
extremely moved'   *Colin Parry yesterday after the death of his son Tim*

GOODBYE TO A FINE LAD

BY ANDREW LOUDON

**IRA bomb victim Timothy Parry's five-day battle for life ended
yesterday with his father at his side.**

**Doctors switched off the 12-year-old's ventilator after his parents, his brother
and his sister had spent two hours saying their goodbyes.**

Final tests had confirmed that Tim, who
suffered devastating injuries in Saturday's
bombing of Warrington, had no brain
activity and was clinically dead.

5 Later Colin Parry, a 37-year-old personnel
director, spoke of his 'fine lad', his final
days and his peaceful death.

He said: 'I am ever so pleased he just
passed away ever so quietly.

10 'The doctors did warn me certain things
can happen when the machine is switched
off, but he was a good lad.

'He just lay there and quietly slipped away –
most unlike himself, because he was

15 normally such a noisy, impudent chap. It
wouldn't have surprised me if he had sat up
and shouted "Geronimo" as he went.

'But he didn't. He went ever so quietly and
it was very peaceful. I have to say I was

20 extremely moved.'

Flowers

Tim was on his way to buy a pair of
Everton football shorts when two bombs
blew apart the cast-iron litter bins in which
they had been placed, killing three-year-

25 old Johnathan Ball and sending shrapnel
scything through more than 50 people.
Tim took the full force of the second device
in the face.

Hope for his recovery had flickered briefly,

30 but Mr Parry and his 35-year-old wife
Wendy knew what was to happen when
they arrived at Liverpool's Walton Centre
for Neurosurgery at 8.30am yesterday.
They had brought their son Dominic, 14,

35 and daughter Abigail, 11, to say goodbye.
All four carried bunches of spring flowers
which they laid beside his bed in the
children's intensive therapy unit.
Tim died physically at 11.20am. Holding

40 his wife's hand, Mr Parry said: 'Wendy
and I, I think, realised yesterday that this
was inevitable although there always lingers
some hope. The really hard part is that on
Saturday the day was unbelievably painful

45 and when we finally found out about Tim
we didn't think he would live the night.
'That was an awful time but hope rose from
then on and Tim seemed capable of beating
this. Because of his efforts, and without

50 really meaning to, we became very opti-
mistic although we didn't say it openly.
'Yesterday morning we had almost reached
the point of believing the tests would be
plain sailing. We really did think he would

55 make it, so yesterday was absolute agony.
'In some ways it was worse than Saturday
because it was then we realised that all
hope had gone. Dr Miles (consultant

surgeon John Miles) did say that miracles
60 can happen and of course you cling to that
and we desperately hoped one would
happen. But, as you now know, it didn't
and Tim has gone.
'Although he has gone, he has not gone
65 really. We have told our other children
everything. They saw Tim before the
machine was switched off and they held
his hand and they were close to him and
that was important to us.
70 'We didn't want Tim to die without Dominic and Abby seeing him and touching
him. There was a nice moment there.
'I stayed with Tim when the machine was
switched off. Wendy – I think rightly –
75 didn't but I did.' [...]
Thanking hospital staff at Liverpool, he
added: 'I know the country was praying
for Tim. It is terrible it never worked.
'We have got to cling to the view that some
80 good will come out of this. The lady in
Ireland who organised the meeting in
Dublin yesterday has our best wishes
because, quite frankly, it's going to take a
lot more people like that to stand up and be
85 counted to make sure other parents don't
have to go through the absolute horror
– and I mean horror – that Wendy and I
have gone through this week.'
Asked if he felt anger towards the IRA, Mr
90 Parry said: 'I honestly don't. It is not
because I am being magnanimous – I just
feel loss for us, Wendy and myself.
'We produced a bloody good kid – one of
three. He was a fine lad. He had his
95 moments and could be a cheeky, impudent
little pup. But he was a great kid, a good
character, and our thoughts are just with
Tim and our family.
'The IRA? I have really got no words for
100 them at all.'

© *Daily Mail, March 26, 1993*
Copyright by Solo

Annotations:
lad – young boy; IRA – Irish Republican Army, A Catholic underground organisation fighting for the independence of Northern Ireland from the U.K.; l.2 devastating – bringing destruction and death; l.3 Saturday's bombing at Warrington – on Sat March 20, 1993, the IRA planted two bombs in dustbins outside a shopping area in Warrington near Liverpool. The two bombs went off killing a three-year-old and seriously injuring more than 40 shoppers, among them Timothy Parry; l.15 impudent – frech; l.17 Geronimo – a possible reference to the warlike Apache chief; l.23 cast-iron litter bin – eiserne Müllcontainer; l.25 shrapnel – metal pieces from a bomb; l.26 scythe – here: flying; l.27 .device – here: bomb; l.33 neurosurgery – Neurochirurgie; l.38 intensive therapy unit – Intensivstation; l.54 plain sailing – uncomplicated; l.55 agony – suffering and pain; l.58/59 consultant surgeon – Chefchirurg; l.80/81 the lady in Ireland – Susan McHugh, 37, from Dublin, started the movement 'Mothers of Ireland`, organised a recent peace rally in Dublin; l.91 magnanimous – großherzig; l.93 bloody – here: extremely ; l.95 cheeky – impudent.

A. Comprehension

As you settle down to work out the comprehension questions on the *Daily Mail* article, review Steps 1–4, page 7 and 8.

Keep in mind that in your answers you must use your own words!

1. When and how did 12-year-old Timothy Parry die? (2 sentences)
2. What made the Walton Centre's doctors in Liverpool take their decision ? (1–2 sentences)
3. How is the moment of Tim dying described by his father Colin Parry? (4 sentences)
4. How is he characterised by his father? (2–3 sentences)
5. What caused Tim's serious condition? (4–5 sentences)
6. Why did the Parrys bring their two other children to say goodbye to their brother? (3 sentences)
7. What does the father describe as the hardest part in the five-day battle for Tim's life? (3 sentences)
8. Does Colin Parry see any positive effects resulting from this sad event? (2 sentences)
9. What does he feel towards the IRA ? (3 sentences)

B. Summary Writing

Step 1   Update your knowledge of **summary technique**. Write down the basic rules of summary writing. In case you can't remember look at page 9.

Info

When asked to summarize the *Daily Mail* article you may wonder where to start. It may appear to you that the *Daily Mail* correspondent "jumps" from fact to fact. Bits of information seem to be scattered over the page. You may have got a point there.

Journalists may disregard the chronology (Reihenfolge) of events or logical text structure in order to maximise the effect on the reader by the unusual arrangement of their material.

A good summary, however, attempts to do just that, i.e. establish some kind of order whether it be chronological, progressive or cause-to-effect.

Step 2   Use this 'skeleton layout' of the *Daily Mail* text for your second reading. As
you go along, elicit key words and key sentences from the text. Fill them
into the structural pattern below. Some entries have already been made.

Quotation: ....

Headline: ....

One-sentence summary: ....
.... yesterday.

Correspondent's report

part one: l. 1 – l. 20

yesterday (key fact)	....
(key fact explained)	final test ....
after Tim's death (eyewitness report)	father speaks out: ....

part two: l. 21 – l. 100

5-day recap of events	5-day battle .... Tim's death 11:20 p.m.
5-day recap: family's feelings	.... Tim gone/not gone
outlook to the future	....

Step 3   The skeleton layout on page 17 follows the way *Daily Mail* correspondent Andrew Loudon has chosen to arrange his "story". Regroup the main points so that they reflect a chronological order.
Jot down key words only.

1. ....   Sat, March 20
   ....
   ....

2. ....   Sun, March 21
   ....
   ....

3. ....   Tue, March 23
   ....
   ....

4. ....   Wed, March 24
   ....
   ....

5. ....   Wed, March 24
   ....
   ....

6. ....   Thur, March 25
   ....
   ....

7. ....   Thur, March 25
   ....
   ....

8. ....   Thur, March 25
   ....
   ....

Step 4 Write a summary of *Goodbye to a Fine Lad* in about 200 words.

How about beginning like this:

"In his article from March 26, 1993, Daily Mail *correspondent Andrew Loudon reports on the Parry family's final farewell to ..."*

C. Comment / Composition

1. To cope with the feelings raging inside her, Mrs Parry decides to start a diary about the five-day battle for Tim's life (March 20 – March 25). Imagine her situation and write some of her entries.

2. One of the Parry kids writes a farewell letter to Tim.

3. Write a letter to the editor of the *Daily Mail* expressing your outrage at the tragic incident that cost Tim his life.

When choosing one (or more) of the above topics for a personal comment of your own, you may go back to Text 1, page 11–13 (How to write a comment) and use the methodical help given there. Consider Steps 1–6.

Topic: *Summary, Choice of Words in a News Report*   **Text 3**

————— **Medicine** —————

Green Light for Gene Therapy

Scientists stand on the brink of a clinical revolution

T he goal is grand and maddeningly difficult to achieve. Ever since Watson and Crick first deciphered the structure of DNA in 1953, doctors have had visions of
5 treating disease not from the outside, with drugs or scalpels, but from the inside, by altering the primal instructions tucked in the nucleus of living cells. Doing so, however, requires scientific techniques of
10 almost unimaginable complexity, and there are legitimate concerns about the risks of inserting new genes into human cells.
After years of debate and lengthy tests with animal subjects, the first human trials are
15 about to begin. Last week two experimental techniques passed a major U.S. government regulatory hurdle, winning approval from the Recombinant DNA Advisory Committee, which reviews genetic-engineering
20 projects for the National Institutes of Health. The official go-ahead from the director of the NIH, as well as a nod from the Food and Drug Administration, is expected to follow within the next few months for at least one
25 of the experiments, clearing the way for human gene treatments as early as this fall. "This is the first step toward what will probably be a medical revolution," said Dr. W. French Anderson, one of the
30 scientists whose proposal was approved. "Millions of patients are going to be helped by this in the future."
The two experiments rely on a technology that has evolved over the past 12 years.

THE PLAN OF ATTACK

In one of the experiments that received approval last week, researchers will use genetically engineered blood cells to fight skin cancer.

GENE SEGMENT

VIRUS

1 The key is a gene that produces a protein that combats tumors. In the first step, this gene will be spliced into the genetic material of a virus.

LYMPHOCYTE BLOOD CELL

Nucleus

Genetic material

2 The virus will be allowed to infect lymphocytes, a type of blood cell, taken from the patient.

3 The lymphocytes with the new gene will be cultured in test tubes so that they multiply into millions.

Cancerous tumor

4 Finally the batch of lymphocytes will be injected into the patient's bloodstream. It is hoped the new protein produced by the lymphocytes will kill tumor cells.

TIME Chart by Steve Hart

35 Each uses a virus to act as a kind of biological taxi to transport a desired gene into the nucleus of human blood cells. In one experiment, a team led by Dr. Steven Rosenberg proposes to treat malignant melanoma,

40 a form of skin cancer, with blood cells that have been genetically altered to transform them into tiny factories for a tumorkilling protein.

The experiment proposed by Anderson is 45 more controversial. He would use gene therapy to treat children who lack a key immune-system enzyme called adenosine deaminase (ADA), leaving them, like the "bubble boy" who lived in a plastic 50 enclosure, vulnerable to every passing germ. Some researchers question the wisdom of performing a novel and potentially dangerous therapy on children, especially since there is already an effective 55 drug treatment. "There are a lot of other diseases without therapies," says Duke University's Dr. Michael Hershfield, an expert on ADA deficiency. "And they're in adults, who can make decisions for 60 themselves."

Thousands of inherited diseases may be linked to the malfunctioning of specific genes. In addition, researchers are dis-covering that nearly every disorder has a 65 genetic component. Last week the National Cancer Institute published two studies suggesting that susceptibility to lung cancer may be associated with a single gene.

But there is no guarantee that gene therapy 70 will be effective against any of these illnesses. Some genes are too big to fit inside the viral taxi. Some would have to be fixed inside the sperm or egg cells, a procedure that raises profound ethical 75 questions about tampering with the biological heritage of future generations. And things could always go wrong. The new genes might not "turn on" inside the body, or they might get misplaced in the gene 80 sequence and rather than fight cancers, start triggering them instead. Ultimately, the only way to see what happens is with carefully designed experiments. As Anderson puts it, "Now we can find out if gene 85 therapy is really going to work."

By Philip Elmer-De Witt.
Reported by Dick Thompson/Washington

Time, August 13, 1990. Copyright 1990 Time Inc.
Reprinted by permission.

Annotations:
l.4 DNA – the acid which carries genetic information in a cell; l.7 primal instructions – ursprüngliche Erbinformationen; l.17 regulatory hurdle – laws established by government; l.18 Recombinant DNA Advisory Committee – Aufsichtsbehörde für Genexperimente in den U.S.A.; l.22 NIH – National Institutes of Health; l.26 fall – AE. for autumn; l.34 evolve – to be developed; l.40 malignant melenoma – bösartiges Karzinom; l.45 controversial – umstritten; l.47 immune system enzyme – chemische Substanz, die das Immunsystem schützt; l.49 bubble boy – boy who has to live in a plastic tent (–bubble) protecting him from the germs in our natural environment; l.52 novel – new; l.58 ADA deficiency – Schwäche des Immunsystems; l.62 malfunctioning – disturbed function; l.67 susceptibility – Empfänglichkeit für eine Krankheit; l.72 viral – adjective of virus; l.75 tamper with – manipulate; l.76 heritage – Erbe; l.81 trigger – start; cause to happen

A. Summary Writing

Working with Text 1 you have entered – successfully we hope – the realm of summary writing. You might pick up what was said there (summary rules!) and continue practising here, this time with a slight difference though. Everybody likes a change, right?

This time most of your preparatory work (Text 1; Steps 1–4) has been done already.

Step 1   Study this 'skeleton' ➡ a graphic illustration of how one of the experiments mentioned in the article is to be conducted. Check the words in the word list below.

Words
one experiment – the plan of attack – blood cells – gene produces protein – fight skin cancer

1. as a first step – splice into a virus

2. then – take blood cells from patient – virus infects lymphocytes

3. next – lymphocytes with new gene – to culture in a test tube – to multiply into millions

4. finally – inject blood cells with gene into bloodstream – hope: protein produced – kills tumor cells

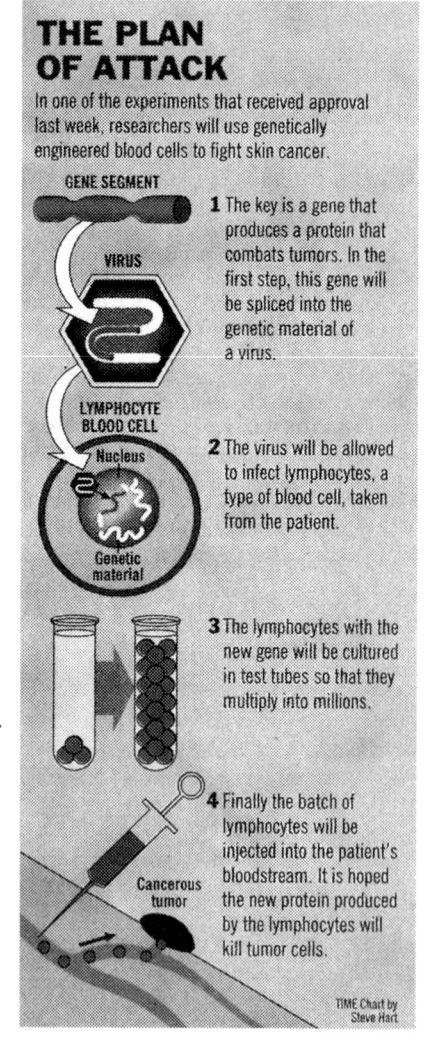

THE PLAN OF ATTACK

In one of the experiments that received approval last week, researchers will use genetically engineered blood cells to fight skin cancer.

GENE SEGMENT

VIRUS

1 The key is a gene that produces a protein that combats tumors. In the first step, this gene will be spliced into the genetic material of a virus.

LYMPHOCYTE BLOOD CELL

Nucleus

Genetic material

2 The virus will be allowed to infect lymphocytes, a type of blood cell, taken from the patient.

3 The lymphocytes with the new gene will be cultured in test tubes so that they multiply into millions.

4 Finally the batch of lymphocytes will be injected into the patient's bloodstream. It is hoped the new protein produced by the lymphocytes will kill tumor cells.

Cancerous tumor

TIME Chart by Steve Hart

Time, August 13, 1990. Copyright 1990 Time Inc. Reprinted by permission.

Step 2   Before getting down to write your summary, you should decide about two more things.

    a. How do you make sure your text is coherent? The vocabulary above helps suggest a **temporal structure**. Be free to use any other kind of pattern (Muster), only be sure to use one!

    b. As the diagram illustrates the experiment itself rather than telling you who conducts it, you should decide to use passive voice throughout.

Step 3   Write a summary of *The Plan of Attack* in about 100–110 words. Do not include the numbering from the illustration if you can help it.
Your summary might begin like this:

The Plan of Attack
"In one of the experiments mentioned in the Time *article (Aug 13, 1990) human blood cells engineered to contain a cancer-fighting gene will be used. ... "*

B. Text Analysis

Time is an American news magazine published on a weekly basis and read all over the world. It addresses the "educated reader" keeping him/her well-informed and up-to-date on political and other themes of topical interest. *Time* considers it important to communicate scientific themes to the average reader.
How does *Time Magazine* achieve this? In order to answer that question let us look at the language mix used by the authors.

How to analyse choice of words in a news report

Info
A good deal of the words and phrases used by the authors in our article belong to everyday language or to what is called the common core of English (Kernbereich des Englischen). That is only to be expected. However, if you read carefully enough, you will come across unusual vocabulary, too.

Examples

decipher DNA   (l.3)
biological taxi   (ll.35/36)
malignant melanoma   (l.39)

What precisely can we do with these examples? Well, how about grouping or classifying them somehow? What type of English do they belong to, which sectors of the English language do they come from?

Examples

word/expression	area of language
a. decipher DNA (l.3/4)	➡ scientific
b. malignant melanoma (l.39)	➡ scientific
c. skin cancer (l.40)	➡ everyday language common core of English
d. biological taxi (ll.35/36)	➡ common core of English metaphorical

It is interesting to note that the authors draw their vocabulary from very different sectors, or levels, of language. They sometimes do so to express the same idea. See b. and c.

Step 1   The task now is to use these categories to group striking words and expressions from our text. As the area of common core is so vast, you need to further subdivide this category according to progress (common core) and risk (common core).

For completing the scheme below read the entire article once again with a keen eye on dominant words and expressions.
Mark them with different colours and group them accordingly.

Major wordfields

progress (common core)	gene therapy (scientific)	risks (common core)
– green light (headline)	– decipher DNA	– maddeningly difficult
– grand goal	– primal instructions	– no guarantee
– human trials	– nucleus of living cells	– profound ethical
– ...	– ...	– questions
– ...	– ...	– ...
– ...	– ...	– ...

Step 2 Study the following paragraph on the authors' **choice of words** in the
Time article and fill in the gaps from the list below:

The *Time* article (Aug. 13, 1990) deals with a hoped for .... for doctors in
.... therapy. This highly complicated medical subject is by no means presented to
a group of .... experts. The magazine's foremost intention being to ....
and update the "................. reader", its authors must keep this fact in mind.
Clearly, they cannot do without a fair amount of scientific vocabulary and
.... This is reflected in the article. A closer look at the authors'
.... reveals that the text .... vocabulary drawn from medicine
and biochemistry. Words such as '..' (l.3),
'.....................................'(l.47) or '.............................' (l.40) appear to dominate
the text. Expressions like '....................' or '......................' recur several times,
which emphasize the article's serious and .... character. On the other hand,
however, the authors use quite a number of expressions and words that can be
.... everyday English or .... Adjective/noun combinations
like 'grand goal'(l.1) or '....................' (l.21), verb phrases such as 'treat a disease'(l.5.)
or '..........................' (l.25) serve to win and maintain the reader's interest and help
him/her to fully grasp the contents. More importantly, ... expressions
('....................', l.35/36; 'green light') are used to popularize the theme for non-
expert readers.
Considering this, one can conclude that the .... serves
the authors' purposes quite well. The article clearly brings home its point.

Vocabulary list:

*biological taxi – blood cells – breakthrough – broad range of vocabulary – choice of
words – classified as – clear the way – common core – decipher the structure of DNA –
educated – gene – immune system enzyme – inform – informative – is rich in – living cells –
metaphorical – official go-ahead – scientific – technical terms*

C. Comment / Composition

By now you are familiar with the way to prepare your case for a personal comment, you know which "rules" to respect and you have quite a few useful phrases and expressions of opinion to choose from when you want to make your comment sound effective. Here is your choice of comment questions for this unit.

1. Gene therapy 'raises profound ethical questions about tampering with the biological heritage of future generations' (ll. 74–76).
   How would you formulate them?

2. Tampering with genetic material should be made illegal and forbidden once and for all.

3. Imagine you were suffering from an illness that doctors propose to treat with gene therapy. Would you give your consent to such an experiment?

Vocabulary helps:

- biotechnology is developing fast
- doctors can now treat/cope with …
- this is a revolution in …
- this is unparalleled in history
- brings genetic health for thousands of …
- however this raises some very thorny (komplizierte) questions
- for example …
- a disease that kills …
- does this mean that we should force anybody who is at risk for …
- there will be a lot of pressure for …
- costly longterm diseases
- should everybody be tested for …?
- no matter what we will do, the impact (Auswirkungen) will be dramatic
- will we want to treat all diseases?
- what will happen when scientists discover …?
- future decisions will be so much more difficult that we need a lot of wisdom
- will we have it?

Topic: *Picture and Words in an Advert*   Text 4

Copyright holder for the Nissan Advertisement on pages 27, 30 are: Advertiser Nissan Europe NV, Agency TBWA/NETH-work, Concept Maarten Boog, Copy Mark Renusch, Photography Ruud Postuma

A. Text Analysis

How to analyse the picture in an advert

This time we propose to study quite a different type of text – a newspaper ad. Text 1 and Text 3 were written to inform the reader on current topics (American youths arming themselves; experimental gene therapy), topics which are interesting and thought-provoking in themselves. A newspaper ad cannot rely on the attractiveness of its theme alone. It must attempt to create an **interest for the reader** and **persuade** him to notice, look and possibly decide to buy.

Step 1   Every picture tells a story. Consequently adverts devote much space to pictures. Take the example above.

Read the following statements on the picture 'Car and Dog'.
Mark them: agree = + ; disagree = – ; don't know = ?

… tells me nothing new.   ☐

… makes me look twice.   ☐

… explains the dog's problem.   ☐

… is quite funny.   ☐

… suggests the dog has a problem.   ☐

… shows the dog thinking it would be nice to
sit in the car.   ☐

… has originality.   ☐

… confuses me (what has a dog to do with
a car anyway?).   ☐

… stirs my imagination.   ☐

… presents a fresh view about cars.   ☐

… joins two different elements in an unusual way.   ☐

… is plain boring.   ☐

… makes me somehow curious.   ☐

Step 2   Take a second look at your favourite choices and jot down your reasons
for each of them.

your choice		your reasons
makes me look twice	➡	because I fail to see its point.
		What is the dog waiting for and why does
		he seem so interested in a car of all things?
....	➡	because ....
....	➡	....
....	➡	....

Step 3   'Skeleton' into text! You know the way it works by now, don't you?
Use your material compiled in Steps 1 and 2 to write a paragraph explain-
ing your personal reactions to the picture *Car and Dog*.

Words

The	picture	presents …	sitting …
	photo	reveals …	waiting …
	snapshot		

It	joins	two different elements,	
	combines	contrasting motives …	and…
	juxtaposes	disparate …	

This	unusual	combination … makes you	look twice at …
	astonishing	alliance …	pause to think about …
	unconventional		ask yourself what …
	atypical		wonder what …

Perhaps the dog …
Apparently …

What	puzzles me is that …
	I fail to see is whether …
	I cannot explain is that …

My idea is that …
My understanding is that …

Besides	the text line seems	to disagree with …
More importantly,	the words appear	to jar with …
		to raise further questions about …

Could it be that …
I could imagine that …

That is a	strange indeed.
	funny …
	bizarre …

Step 4   On page 30 you find the complete *Nissan* advert at last. Read it twice, very carefully. Find out whether the text can satisfy your curiosity aroused by the picture (= persuade you!) and provide answers to the "mystery" of the picture.

When you're looking for a wagon, consult an expert.

In your search for a new family car, you read all the car magazines. Ask all your neighbours questions. All your colleagues, too.

5 Perhaps you forgot to consult the expert that's by your side all the time. The one that always sits in the back.

Place him before a Primera Wagon. He'll just sit there, admiring the beautiful, 10 smooth shape. Until you open the hatch door. Watch how he easily slips through the wide tailgate. Notice him sniffing the carpet. (Don't worry, it's stain resistant).

Now get behind the powered steering 15 wheel. Yes, you.

Fire up the available 2.0-litre, 16-valve engine and soon your dog's tail will start wagging to and fro. Once on the road, even he'll have to strain to hear wind and road 20 noise.

Open the electric windows, he'll stick his head out to check the windflow, no doubt. But don't test the ABS until he's safely inside.

25 Now that everything has been checked, he'll stretch out in the back. Where thanks to a unique rear suspension, the floor is completely flat.

Pampered with all this comfort, he'll 30 fall asleep. Consider it a sign of approval.

Primera Wagon.
The best friend of the family.

---

smooth shape – harmonische äußere Form; hatch door/tailgate – Heckklappe; warranty – Garantie; stain resistant carpet – fleckenabstoßender Bodenteppich; powered steering wheel – Servolenkung; 2.0 litre 16-valve engine – 2.0 l. 16-Ventiler; rear suspension – Hinterradaufhängung.

How to analyse the words in an advert

If the ad photographer has successfully caught the reader's eye, the text writer cannot afford to lose it again. He must likewise strive to fuel the reader's interest and persuade the prospective buyer to read the message. The ad text must satisfy the reader's curiosity, it must "taste fresh". Who likes stale food (for thought)?

The text, simply, has to be …   – noticeable   – compelling   – appealing
                                 – surprising   – striking   – funny.

It has to meet at least some of these criteria, preferably all of them. How does the Nissan text writer achieve this? The answer can be found through: **Word Study**.

Step 1   To help narrow their choice down the family is advised to "consult a car tester": their best friend, the family dog!
How does the "tester" proceed to take in, check and pronounce his judgement on the quality of the product, a technically designed machine? Study the choice of words in our text. Find relevant words and expressions to complete the following table.

the car tester's actions	the car's technical equipment	
sit and admire	smooth shape (form)	
....	....	(......)
....	....	(......)
....	....	(......)
....	....	(......)
his final judgment	....	(......)

Step 2   Surprising? – Déja Vu? – Funny? – Or what?

- Having compiled and sorted out your word material you are in a position now to draw your conclusions.
- Explain the car tester's peculiar testing method. (Is he up to his job? What distinguishes him from a regular car tester?)
- Point out what the dog-idea adds to the atmosphere of the text. (Compare to the product itself and what it stands for).
- Contrast the different areas (= "worlds") that the words and expressions are drawn from.
(What does that mean? What kind of balance is achieved?)
- Comment on the overall effect created by the main advertising idea and the choice of "dog-related" words in our text.
(Does the text "taste fresh"? Is it persuasive?)

Step 3   Read this essay on the persuasiveness of a similar *Nissan Primera*
            advert written by 11th-grader Laurenz Voss from Troisdorf near Bonn.

*Regarding the dog sitting in the boot most of the readers stop reading the newspaper
or magazine and start reading the advert. That is exactly the intention of the author.
So as a first step the dog is used to catch the reader's eye. But the dog is employed in
a couple of ways as well.*

*So the reader is made to draw a parallel between the dog (especially this kind of
dog) as a family friend and the "Primera Wagon" as a family car. This suggestion is
emphasised by the expression "Primera Wagon the best friend of the family".
Furthermore the author makes use of the dog as a car tester.*

*A closer look at the reveals that the text contains expressions drawn from the fields
of technique, comfort and vocabulary that describes the family values.*

*To begin with the author addresses the reader by using a couple of words from the
area of technique, e.g. when the "two-litre 16 valve engine" and the "unique rear
suspension" are mentioned. Thus the reader gets a first positive impression. In the
following the author peppers his text with expressions drawn from the field of comfort. So it is implied that one can "make oneself completely at home".*

*Furthermore the "car-tester" dog feels "relaxed" like never before. And eventually
the dog feels so much at ease that you cannot get him out. These are further important implications.*

*As a third step the dog tests the family values by "paying a visit to the luxurious
passenger area". Sniffing at the "stain resistant carpet of the huge luggage compart-
ment" he agrees to it. This has the effect of showing the reader the family values of
the car. ...*

*So, all in all one can say that the author has got a vocabulary rich in implications
that is well suited for his purpose. But apart from the lexical choices there is the
marvellous idea of the dog. He is used to catch the reader's eye, to make the reader
draw a parallel between the family dog and the car and to make the technique
familiar.*

Considering all this, the text has to be regarded as a very persuasive one.

Step 4   This fine example is to encourage you to write your own comments on
            non-fictional texts.
            Go through the essay again. Collect ten useful expressions and phrases
            for language analysis. Add them to your active vocabulary.

Topic: *Choice of Words and Syntax in an Advert*   Text 5

A. Activity

Step 1   This picture tells another story, doesn't it?
Tell the story from your personal point of view by commenting on the
effect that the photo has on you (120 words).

You may want to turn back to Text 4, Steps 1–3 as your guide-line for this
task.

Words

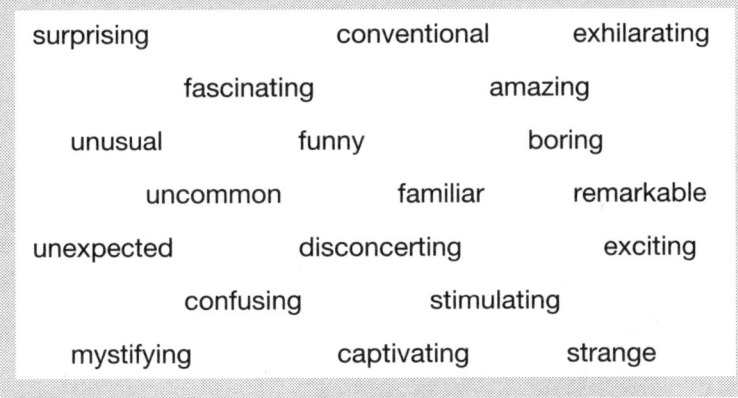

surprising   conventional   exhilarating
        fascinating   amazing
    unusual   funny   boring
        uncommon   familiar   remarkable
unexpected   disconcerting   exciting
        confusing   stimulating
    mystifying   captivating   strange

Step 2   Here is the complete picture then. It may come as a surprise that there are
in fact two similar pictures to whet, not the cat's, but your appetite.
Take your time to study the two photos carefully. Notice in what they
differ.

Abbildungen S. 33,
34, Text S. 35, 36
© Philips Electronics
NV

Step 3   Read the two following advert texts. As you read, try to imagine which text fits which of the two photos best.

Text 1

Now Philips offers a notebook PC for the free spirit.

One that gives you maximum inde-pendence, because we have concentrated
5 **more power and speed into less space.**

The new 386SX, for example, weighs just 3.1 kg and has a footprint that's smaller than a sheet of A4 paper.

And, as with all of our PCs, it comes
10 **complete with a unique feature.**

The Philips name.

A name synonymous with superior design, outstanding quality and sophis-ticated technology, such as CD-ROM which
15 **will be the heart of future PCs.**

All backed up by a truly professional after-sales service co-ordinated by our wide network of specialist dealers.

So wether you require a slimline
20 **notebook PC, a powerful desktop or an advanced tower PC, you can always depend on expert support.**

Offering you the peace of mind that only a company with worldwide resources
25 **can realistically provide.**

On balance, a Philips notebook PC is a great investment in your future.

Philips PCs. The breed for business.

Annotations:
l.7 footprint – here: needs space; l.13 sophisti-cated – hochentwickelt; l.14 CD-ROM – Read-Only-Memory, a disk with an immense amount of data that you can use.

Text 2

If you're hungry for success, get your teeth into a Philips PC.

Whatever your business requirements, we can provide you with the perfect
5 combination of speed and power.

Our 386 range, for example, has been endorsed by the leading authority in networking for their ability to serve large and expanding networks.

10   And, as with all of our PCs, they come complete with a unique feature.

The Philips name.

A name synonymous with superior design, outstanding quality and sophis-
15 ticated technology, such as CD-ROM which will be the heart of future PCs.

All backed up by a truly professional after-sales service co-ordinated by our network of specialist dealers.

20   So wether you require a powerful desktop PC, an advanced deskside or one of our slimline notebook PCs, you can always depend on expert support.

Offering you the peace of mind that
25 only a company with worldwide resources can realistically provide.

If you're investing in the future, a Philips PC will help to give your business more bite.

30   Philips PCs. The breed for business.

PHILIPS

Annotations:
l.3 requirements – Erfordernisse; l.6 range – Reichweite; l.7 endorse – back up; l.21 deskside – tower PC.

Easy job, true? For one thing, you will have stumbled over the first lines in each of the two texts. While Text 1 speaks of a 'notebook PC', which is displayed in picture 2, Text 2 mentions a desktop 'Philips PC' like the one that is partly shown in picture 1. For another, talking about the range of Philips computers available, each text chooses a different order (ll.20–24, ll.19–22). Compare (1) <u>notebook PC</u>, (2) desktop, and (3) advanced tower PC in Text 1 with (1) <u>desktop PC</u>, (2) deskside, and (3) slimline notebook PC in Text 2.

Those are not the only clues (Indizien), though. There is more for you to find out.

B. Text Analysis

How to analyse the choice of words in an advert

Step 1   Turn to both texts again watching out for text differences this time. In order to contrast textual details fill in the following table.

Do not go for the various types of computers advertised. You have covered that aspect in Steps 2 and 3.

Text 1 (notebook PC)	Text 2 (Philips PC)
perfect balance of power and size (headline)	be more power hungry (headline)
the free spirit (l.2)	....
....	....
....	....
....	....
....	....
....	....
....	....
....	....
....	....

Step 2   To prove your point beyond doubt you will have to look at the cat pictures again. The photos show the cat in two remarkably different situations. Examine then the word material you have collected in the table above with a close eye on correspondences (Entsprechungen) between texts and pictures.

Answer the following questions:

– What is striking ? Do you believe this is accidental?

– In what way do the words in each text "capture" the moment and the cat's activities?

– What appears to have been the author's intention in doing so?

The slight but unmistakeable textual differences you have discovered seem to be related **to the cat** in the first place, or do they?

We can find a clear answer when we consider that words do not only have obvious **denotations** but more or less hidden **connotations** as well.

Info

The English language with its **rich vocabulary** is an infinite source that a writer can tap to produce a fresh and stimulating text. A lot depends on his skilful **handling of the words** available to him. The writer can draw from almost any area of English, whether common core or colloquial, whether literal or metaphorical, or any other variety of English. He can virtually **play with words** or, rather, with the various **levels of meaning** a particular word has in order to achieve a fresh effect.

Take **denotation** and **connotation**, for example.
"Denotation is the accepted meaning of a word. Connotation is the implication of (Anspielung auf) something more than the accepted or primary meaning; it refers to the qualities, attributes, and characteristics implied or suggested by the word. From its plain meaning and its sound the word may have associations, images, echoes, impressions … and create wider ripples of meaning in the mind of the responsive reader."
(A.F. Scott, Current Literary Terms. Macmillan, London, 1965)

Example

The word 'mouse' denotes = literally means an animal, a small rodent (Nagetier), typically living on seeds and nuts.
In addition, 'mouse' can be used to address a woman or child you love;
'mouse' can also be a useful part of your computer equipment, something that allows you move the cursor on your screen.
(The New Shorter Oxford English Dictionary, Clarendon Press, Oxford 1993)

Step 3   Go over your wordlist on page 37 again. Check the words in your dictionary and note down your 'echoes', i.e. your associations and understanding
in different contexts.

word/phrase	denotation (cat's world)	connotation = echo (computer world)
hungry for success	cat = hungry; natural mouse-hunter; preys on mice;	businessman interested in effective office work; eager to achieve some- thing;
get your teeth into	catch a mouse; bite mouse to kill it;	
....	....	....
....	....	....
....	....	....
....	....	....

Step 4   Have you now got second thoughts about the author's choice of words?
Write a few paragraphs on the denotative and the connotative use of
vocabulary in the Philips adverts. Use the words on page 40.

How to analyse syntax in an advert

As we said earlier, a successful advert must catch the reader's eyes, it must then satisfy
his curiosity and maintain his interest by persuading him to stay and "digest" the
message of the text. We have seen how photographer and copy-writer attempt to
achieve that.

Words, however skilfully they are chosen by the advert writer, do not stand isolated.
Words alone do not "make a text". They have to be connected to form **sentences**.
Sentences are "woven into" a text! (Syntax).

Words

Dealing with a topic as widely advertised as …, the writer has to strike a fresh
The … advert attempts this by …   note.
This is true for both examples.

The two adverts reveal a | carefully chosen vocabulary.
                         | skilfully
The author | uses
           | employs …

Quite a few … are related to the product itself.
We can trace such words as '……'
This, however, is what you would find in …

To make it more persuasive | the author | intersperses his text with
Besides | the texter | peppers
This is further enhanced because | mixes his vocabulary with

                    | words/expressions   rich in | implications
                    | terms | connotations.

We can | trace   quite a few which are used in a figurative metaphorical sense.
       | observe

The | word | denotes
    | phrase | literally means

In | our   context, however, … it | hints at
   | the given | suggests   that | other examples
                                          | implies   that | further
                                          | echoes | similar

                                                                  are to be quoted.

Expressions like "…"   have a | funny | overtone
                                 | witty | note
                                 | amusing
                          | address the reader's imagination
                          | maintain
                          | sustain   the reader's interest
                          | satisfy

The most | appropriate example | occurs   in ll. … where …
         | ingenious | can be found
         | striking

Info

Sentences can be – statements, questions or commands
– main clauses or dependent clauses
– compound clauses (= main clause + dependent clause)
– short or long
– simple or complex
– complete or incomplete
– connected or unconnected

Brush up your grammar with a short review of sentences and clauses. You will be surprised to find how many different kinds there are.

Step 1 Here is a random selection of sentence structures from the Philips Text 1 (Notebook PC!). Try to group these examples using the table below. Put them in the right slots.

The Philips name. (l.11)
So whether you require a slimline notebook PC, a powerful desktop or an advanced tower PC, you can always depend on expert support. (ll.19–22)
Now Philips offers a notebook PC for the free spirit. (ll.1–2)

total number	type of sentence	example
	incomplete = elliptic clause	....
	short complete main clause	....
	longer "and"-linked main clause	....
	question	
	command	....
	compound clause	....
	(main + dependent)	....

Step 2 Go back to our text; identify the sentences one by one counting their total in column 1. Write down an example of each new type of sentence you find.

Step 3 Complex? – Simple? – Sloppy? – Just right or what?

Having compiled and grouped the sentence structures you are now in a position to look at your results and draw conclusions.

– As regards the author's syntactic choices, are there any noticeable preferences (complete/incomplete; main/dependent; compound) ?

– Which types of sentence structures are apparently underrepresented, which is/are missing altogether?

– Characterize the author's syntactic choices in general (tendency: complex or simple sentences; long, medium or short clauses; connected or unconnected sentences).

– Comment on the overall effect achieved with this particular style (written or spoken English; formal or rather colloquial English; persuasive or not?).

– Can you account for possible reasons that may have led the author to choose his sentences so deliberately (reader's expectations; time angle; purpose of the text?)

Write two or three paragraphs using the above questions as a guide-line. (120–150 words.)

Words

From the start the | text writer | tries to establish a close relationship …
| author | addresses the reader by …

A look at his | syntactic choices | reveals   that
| preferred sentence structures | discloses

… sentences
… structures | dominate the text.
… clauses | prevail in the text.

One feature that | characterizes his style of writing is the … | type of clause
| is typical of | sentence structure

… sentences | occur   so often that we can | characterize
| recur | assess
| mark

| snappy | lengthy
his style as | informal | interesting
| formal | clumsy
| colloquial | boring
| spoken | spontaneous

By comparison
It is | striking that | underrepresented
| interesting to note that   … are | scarce
Quite surprisingly, | missing altogether

This is perhaps | due to
| owing to   … because he | must not bore
There is no question | cannot afford to lose
Undoubtedly | must maintain

On the whole | textwriter | tends to
Considering the prospective reader   the | author | prefers   …
In sum | copywriter | chooses
| favours

sentences which | create | an effect of
| achieve | the effect that
| serve | his purposes quite well.

Topic: *Line of Thought in a Newspaper Comment*   **Text 6**

END THE BLOODY VIOLENCE ... NOW

● OUTRAGED Dublin mother Susan McHugh united all Ireland this week when she pleaded for an end to terrorist slaughter in the wake of bloody Warrington.

● Susan, 37, organised a Dublin peace rally. Thousands turned up. Yesterday, on the day Tim died, four Catholics were mown down in Ulster. This is Susan's reaction.

FIVE more people died because of terrorism yesterday – five more wasted lives.

5 We, the ordinary people of Ireland, are sickened by the never-ending cycle of violence.

Our hearts go out to 10 Tim's family. Our hearts go out to the families of the four Catholic workmen brutally murdered in Derry.

15 The whole of Ireland mourns. The killing has to stop.

Terrorism, whether committed by the IRA or 20 Loyalists, does nothing more than cause more misery in a land sickened by bloodshed.

The people of Ireland 25 are disgusted by these atrocities.

This week, thousands of people joined with me in Dublin in expressing their 30 outrage.

I now hope everyone in Ireland will come out and show their unequivocal disapproval.

35 The politicians on both sides must stop burying their heads in the sand and start talking.

There must be a compromise. 40 There must be some solution to stop the violence.

The people of Ireland will never forget John-45 athan Ball or Tim Parry.

The IRA had no right to take their lives in our name. The terrorists do not represent us.

50 No society can condone the slaughter of children or the slaughter of men on their way to work.

The IRA must lay down 55 their arms NOW in the name of humanity. The Loyalist terrorists must do likewise.

Three thousand have 60 died because of the Ulster troubles.

May they rest in peace. But surely, in the name of God, enough is enough. 65 The time for reconciliation is here.

Daily Mirror, March 26, 1994

Annotations:
outraged – empört, eintrüstet; bloody Warrington – reference to the incident of Text 2; peace rally – Friedensdemonstration; mown down – killed brutally; l.6. sickened – veursacht uns Übelkeit; l.23 bloodshed – Blutvergießen; l.26 atrocities – Greueltaten; l.33/34 unequivocal disapproval – eindeutige Mißbilligung; l.50 condone – forgive; l.57 Loyalist terrorists – Protestants loyal to the British Crown; l.65 reconciliation – Versöhnung.

A. Text Analysis

How do you respond to reports of acts of violence in the papers or on TV, like the tragedy of twelve-year-old Timothy Parry (Text 2, *Goodbye to a Fine Lad*)?

Shock? – Indifference? – Outrage? – Sympathy? – Thank God, I'm German?

When dealing with Text 2 you may have written a 'Letter to the Editor'. If so, remember that letter and compare it to the text by Susan McHugh, published in the *Daily Mirror* on March 26, 1993.

Info
A text that puts forth a personal view convincingly depends – more perhaps than any other kind of text – on its **unity of thought** (gedankliche Geschlossenheit). Even if Susan McHugh's personal comment on the unsolved situation in Northern Ireland is a very emotional and spontaneous one –it appeared one day after the death of 12-year-old Timothy Parry – and even though she is not a professional writer, she follows a clear **line of thought**.
To achieve this commentators like her often follow a clearly defined pattern. Some of the most common compositional patterns are, for example, **listing**, **progressive** or **antithetical** text structuring.

Structuring Texts

Listing	method:	enumerating and, perhaps, numbering of facts, ideas, arguments
	effect:	clarity and coherence through parallel arrangement and, possibly, numerical order
Progressive	method:	using a clearly defined starting point; developing in a cause-to effect or problem-solution arrangement
	effect:	clarity through unity, logical coherence
Antithetical	method:	contrasting and juxtaposing of facts, ideas, arguments
	effect:	clarity and emphasis through comparison and contrast

How to analyse the line of thought in a newspaper comment

Step 1 Read the text again carefully to get an idea of its structural outline. Mark
your text (introduction? main part? conclusion?).

Step 2 What you have now is a very rough division of the text. Any good text is, in
a way, "composed" like that.
Take a second look. Susan McHugh uses what can be called a frame to
introduce and to conclude her comment.
Here is the first part of the frame, find the counterpart (here: the
conclusion) and state in what way she "progresses".

Introduction:

Five more people died	*Fact*
because of terrorism –	*+*
five more wasted lives.	*Opinion*

We, the ordinary people
of Ireland, are sickened by
the never-ending cycle
of violence.

Conclusion:

	Fact
....	*+*
	Opinion
....	*+*
	???

Step 3 A frame holds the full picture, here the main part of the text. Subdivide the
main part (ll.18–58) as you think fit. This will help you to see which two
fundamentally different types of reaction the author expresses.

A closer look at the choice of words (verbs!) she
employs can guide you.
Complete the table on the next page.

verbs:		area of human understanding:
are sickened	expresses	outrage, anger, rage
hearts go out		sympathy
mourns		despair, hopelessness
....		....
....		....
....		....
....		....
....		....
....		....
....		....

Step 4 Having understood the two different kinds of reaction, answer the following questions:

– Why do you think the author arranges both lines of thinking in that order?

– How does she proceed in paragraphs 2–4?

– Why does she renew her condemnation of the brutal acts committed by the IRA (ll.24–26, 50–53)?

– How does she arrange her thoughts in her second line of argument?

Step 5 Use the information on the structure of texts given above and decide which pattern(s) the author makes use of: listing, progressive, or antithetical?
Write a fairly long paragraph in which you describe how the author Susan McHugh "composes" her text.

On the next page you find some vocabulary to help you.

Words

In her comment the | author | voices her …
| text | expresses …
| writer | discloses …

The text | divides into … paragraphs, most of them consisting of sentences,
| breaks into…
| falls into…

no longer than …
very short and compact.

To establish | thematic coherence | she uses a leitmotif technique
| a clear line of thought | she employs …

She | repeatedly … (l. …)
| often …
| frequently …

Moreover   she makes use of a frame
More importantly,

She begins with … and, | at the end,   she returns to …
| in the concluding paragraph,

The argument proper | is a sequence of …
The main part | can be understood as a two-pronged reaction.

This a … structure in itself, as she moves from … to …

In both | parts | she combines …
| units | she prefers … a … pattern.

This becomes most | clear   when she … | lists …
This is | evident | enumerates …
| apparent

The way she arranges her | demands, | at the end … | proves …
| pleas | at the last one, | suggests …
| implies …

B. Comment/Composition

1. If you chose to write your Letter to the Editor when dealing with Text 2 (page 19), read it again. Revise it using some of the compositional ideas you learned in this unit and write a second version. Why not use some of Susan McHugh's phrases and expressions, too?

2. Read other articles from the British or American Press. Pick a problem outlined there to write an "angry" comment on it.

3. Compose a personal comment that takes up a problem in our country you have heard or read about (Violence against foreigners in Germany? Growing violence at your school?) to voice your outrage and protest.

Girls do better without the boys

by Enid Castle

A referendum among parents on the subject of co-education versus single sex some years ago came up with a clear
5　result: they wanted co-education for their sons but single-sex for their daughters. How wise.

The first criterion for choosing a school must be its suitability for the child. Parental
10　convenience (the greater ease of visiting if all children are in the same school, for example), parental nostalgia (father's desire to see his children follow him to the old school) and parental ambition, whether
15　academic or social, must be secondary considerations. However, I urge parents at least to consider the single-sex option.

It is no accident that many of today's most successful women were educated in girls'
20　schools. There is now much evidence, including examination results, to indicate that girls and probably boys do better if taught separately.

Younger girls arriving at Cheltenham from
25　mixed schools frequently claim that the boys in their classes were noisy. What they really mean is that the boys claimed and received a disproportionate amount of the teacher's attention. By and large, as they
30　grow through adolescence, girls are conscientious, keen to learn and keen to receive praise. In a mixed classroom, most will retreat to the sidelines and the boys will dominate. The older girl may compete
35　with the boys; on the other hand she may well be reluctant to appear to outdo them, particularly if she wishes to attract.

In a single-sex situation, everything is provided to encourage girls and there are
40　no inhibitions. All subjects, all careers, all resources and all activities are available to them alone. The headmistress of an infant school tells me that in se-
45　parate groups, boys and girls play happily and in a similar fashion with Lego. When together the girls stand back and the boys grab the wheels. The same kind of thing happens at a later stage.

50　It is often pointed out that men and women work together in adult life. Women, the argument goes, have to compete in a man's world, and so they might as well get used to it early on. For many girls, however, this
55　means that they would never build the confidence required for that competition. Only in a girls' school are they likely to see at least as many women in senior positions as men.

60　In mixed schools boys are likely to take a greater share of responsibility and provide more leaders unless this is carefully controlled. This is particularly so where girls are in a minority. In a girls' school, the
65　girls will take all the positions of leadership. The opportunities will not have to be shared or competed for with boys, confidence will be engendered in the girls and other girls will benefit from their example.

70　What of the social side of education? Don't girls from single-sex boarding schools run wild or get struck dumb when they go on to university and out into the working world? If that was once true, how things have
75　changed. Even in boarding schools, girls have plenty of opportunities to meet the opposite sex. They are allowed out and joint functions are arranged with neighbouring schools.

80　No head of a girls' school today wishes to cloister her or his charges, but it is perhaps as well to remember the maxim: "Girls

when they reach puberty think about love while boys think about sex." This genera-
85 lisation has just about enough truth in it to make teenage girls, exposed constantly to mixed company, very vulnerable. Of course, they will form relationships with boys, but in a girls' school they have the
90 secure freedom of a place of their own to which they can retreat and the chance to divorce their work from the social pressures they meet away from the classroom.

Girls' schools encourage pupils to develop
95 their talents and to seek careers in the professions, industry and commerce. The girls excel academically and often combine examination success with high standards in art, music and sport.

100 They leave as confident young women, able to take their places in universities and in the world of work with the belief that everything is possible for them.

**Enid Castle is principal of
Cheltenham Ladies' College**

The Sunday Times, October 4, 1992
© *Enid Castle/Times Newspaper Ltd. 1992*

Annotations:
l.1 referendum – Umfrage; l.9 suitability – the fact that it must be good for the child; l.9/10 parental convenience – what parents find suitable; l.15/16 secondary consideration – of less importance; l.24 Cheltenham – fairly small town northwest of London; l.28 disproportionate – unusually large; l.37 attract – here: be attractive to boys; l.40 inhibition – feelings of fear and embarrassment; l.68 engender – instil in; l.72 struck dumb – unable to act normally; l.80 head – headmaster or - mistress; l.81 cloister her or his charges – keep s.b. like in monastery

A. Text Analysis

How to analyse the line of thought in a newspaper comment

As a highschool student in Germany you probably attend a co-ed school, where girls and boys "mix" and where they are taught together. There are, as you know, schools where girls and boys are educated separately. Are you satisfied with the type of school you go to or would you favour separate schools for girls and boys?
The article on that subject, written by the headmistress of Cheltenham Ladies' College, appeared in the *Sunday Times*, Oct.4, 1992.

Step 1   Read through the text without interruption trying to understand the author's standpoint.

Step 2   Use the structural outline of the *Sunday Times* article (below) for your
second reading. As you go along, elicit (heraussuchen) key words and key
sentences from the text and fill them in.

given fact (ll.1–7)   ....

author's main   ....

thesis (ll.8–23)   ....

evidence   In a mixed classroom   In a single-sex situation
(ll.24–99)
                 ....
                                                      ↔ ....
                 ....

                 In mixed schools   In a girls' school

                 ....
                                                      ↔ ....
                 ....

                                                   ... but in a girls' school

                 ....
                                                      ↔ ....
                 ....

author's thesis

confirmed   ....

(ll.100–104)   ....

Step 3   Review the information on text composition on page 45.

Step 4   Having updated your knowledge of text composition, you are now
prepared to answer the following questions:

  – Does Enid Castle follow the familiar pattern of Introduction – Main Part –
    Conclusion?

  – Where does the author deal with the subject in general, where does she
    go into particulars?

- How would you describe the overall pattern of her comment: listing, progressive, or antithetical? (see Info, Text 6, page 45)

- Can you define how she arranges her thoughts in the main part?

- To what extent does the author make use of two different patterns in her comment?

Step 5 Write a fairly detailed paragraph in which you describe how the author Enid Castle "composes" her text.

Words

| In her | comment
article | the author | expresses her view of …
states the case for … |

| The text | divides into …
breaks into …
falls into … | main parts,
major sections, | which can be described as … |

| The author | starts off with …
begins with … |

| She then | continues with
carries on with | what can be called … |

| … by | discussing
comparing | the pros and cons of …
the advantages and disadvantages of … |

| In her conclusion
In the two concluding paragraphs | | she returns to her central …
she rejoins her main … |

| … | confirming it …
reinforcing it | from a general point of view. |

Throughout she develops her thoughts …ly.

| The | argumentation,
main part in itself | however, is | structured ....ly
arranged ....ly. |

| Castle | contrasts …
juxtaposes … | effectively. |

B. Comment/Composition

How to write an argumentative text (= personal comment)

Step 1   Read Castle's comment carefully again. Mark the passages that you feel strongly about (= disagree to).

Step 2   Collect your points of objection in a list. Note down your counter arguments.

Example

Most (girls) retreat to the sidelines; *boys dominate*	←→	*many girls are self-assured, too; they know how to get their teacher's attention and can speak out for themselves*
....	←→	....
....	←→	....
....	←→	....

Step 3   Make up your mind how you want to structure your comment.

Why not try and use the way Enid Castle has arranged her thoughts as a model?

1. introduction:	– given fact
	– main thesis
2. development	– argumentation (antithetical)
3. conclusion	– main thesis confirmed

To make your comment sound convincing and to "bring home" your arguments you will need "argumentative" sentence structures and phrases. Go through the following helps and select the sentences and expressions you plan to use in your text.

Sentence links to express …

… **reason**:   therefore, that is why, because, as   (e.g. *Boys and girls will have to work together in later life. Therefore they should be taught together.*)

… **condition**:   if, unless   (e.g. *Girls do better if they are taught separately.*)

… **concession**:   although, even though, despite the fact that   (e.g. *Although boys get more attention from teachers, girls do equally well in the academic subjects.*)

… **result**:   consequently, thus, as a result   (e.g. *Women have to compete in a man's world. Consequently they have to get used to it early on.*)

Phrases to …

… agree/contradict s.b.'s view:

– I absolutely agree to …
– I agree, and in fact one might go as far as to say …
– Certainly that is true but on the other hand …

– I simply disagree to …
– There is no way I can agree to …
– I can see that … but surely …
– I see the author's point but still …

… express one's doubt/certainty:

– I wonder if …
– There is no question that …
– … is a fact nobody can deny
– It is a fact that …
– It is plain to see that …
– … is an idea everybody has to accept

– I cannot really believe that …
– It cannot be denied that …
– … is a point that does not convince me at all
– It stands to reason that …
– It is safe to say that …

Step 4   'Separate education will not help'. Write a personal comment in response to Enid Castle's *Sunday Times* article.

The Routine

His first stint of penal labour came that evening. It was the pointless task of picking up all the loose stones he could find in the vicinity of the House and stacking them in
5 a particular place. He was warned that he would be under observation from the window of the Prefects' Room and that he had better put his back into it. The job was tiring as well as boring. When the bell
10 rang for bedtime he felt utterly exhausted. He undressed, washed and brushed his teeth, and climbed into bed as the lights went out. He could sleep and forget things for a few hours.
15 The noise of feet at the far end of the dormitory came as he was drifting into sleep. He realized vaguely what it must be – senior boys out on the Routine. Not coming for him: he was still a long way
20 short of the three weeks' grace new boys were given. He thought of D'Artagnan again but was even less moved to follow his example. He had enough troubles of his own. Then footsteps approached and
25 lights flashed in his eyes. He sat up.

Two of them had torches, another a portable lumoglobe which he put on top of Rob's locker. There were seven or eight; it was difficult to be sure in the semi-
30 darkness. One said:

"You're a disgrace, Randall. Isn't that true?"

They were probably on their way to some victim. If he humoured them they
35 might go on.

"Yes," he said.

"Yes what?"

"Yes, sir."

"That's better. Repeat after me: 'I know
40 I am a disgrace and I am ashamed of myself.'"

Rob repeated the words mechanically. The boy said:

"I ask the House for punishment because
45 I know I deserve it."

"I've been punished," Rob said. "A month of extra duties."

"Not enough. Not enough for bringing dirty germy books into the House. And
50 that was School punishment, anyway. What you need is House punishment. Isn't it?" Rob did not reply. "Dumb insolence. That makes it worse. Looks as though he needs the Routine. A special Routine."
55 There was no point, Rob thought, in saying anything. He stared up silently at the faces that surrounded his bed.

"On the other hand you're not supposed to get the Routine till you've been here
60 three weeks. And you've admitted you're ashamed of yourself. We might let things go for the time being. Just show you really are ashamed, really sorry for being so disgusting. Get out of bed and get down
65 and kiss our feet. Starting with mine."

He still stared at them. His tormentor said:

"What about it, Randall?"

Rob shook his head. "No."
70 "You're going to regret that. All right. We apply the Routine."

Rob struggled but they pinioned him quite easily. Their faces grinned at him, ugly in the light from the lumoglobe. One
75 said: "The hammer? Knock a bit of decency into him?"

They liked the idea. The hammer that was produced was not very big and the head was not metal but hard rubber. It was
80 swung in front of his face for some moments then tapped, fairly sharply, against his forehead. The feeling was more

unpleasant than painful. The tapping went on in a steady rhythm. After a time it
85 began to hurt. He winced, and one of them said:

"We seem to be getting through. Ready to kiss our feet yet?" He shook his head and the hammer landed in a different place.
90 "We'd better keep on, then."

Soon it was hurting a lot. He remembered Perkins' advice to yell a bit; but he could not bring himself to do it any more than he could have gone down on his knees to
95 them. He gritted his teeth and turned his head slightly. The hammer hit him in another place, a small relief but one that did not last.

The pain was one big ache with smaller
100 sharper jabs exploding into it. He was less aware of the voices and faces; his mind concentrated on the hurt. It went on and on, a savage unending nightmare. He thought he was going to faint and hoped he
105 would, but the pain drew him back. In the end, involuntarily, he cried out, in a scream of agony. The tapping stopped. Someone said:

"O.K. for now. We'll carry on the
110 treatment tomorrow night."

The lumoglobe was picked up. The voices and footsteps went away down the dormitory. Rob's head ached violently. Sleep was far away. Tomorrow night …
115 And the night after? Once they had started there seemed no reason why they should ever stop.

He tried to think objectively though the ache in his head made that difficult. He
120 would be here until school leaving age, seventeen. Four years. Even if the bullying stopped there were all the other things. No home to go back to, no privacy, no books. The place was bad enough in itself: to get
125 used to it would be even worse. Better being tortured than turning into something like the torturers.

But if he managed to get away, where could he go? His aunt the Sheffield Conurb
130 was a long way off and there was no reason to think she would help him. The Kennealys were nearer. But there was no hope there, either. If Mr Kennealy had not been willing to have him before, he would
135 certainly not do so when it would involve trouble with the authorities over someone who had run away from a State Boarding School.

What else? Try to live on his own
140 somehow? But how? It might be possible to dodge the police for a week or two, sleeping in the open or in derelict houses, but he could not do that for long. The little money he had would quickly run out, and
145 there would be no way of getting more except by joining one of the criminal gangs of the underworld. And they probably wouldn't want him either.

One could not hide among the crowds of
150 ordinary people. Everyone had a particular place in society, a routine by which he could be identified. There was no conceal-ment in the teeming streets of the Conurbs. It was hopeless to imagine it.

155 The Conurbs … He sat up in bed, and his head hurt still more. The idea was shocking, unthinkable by the standards of the world he knew, but at the same time exciting. His mother had come from the County to the
160 Conurb. Was it possible dare he think of reversing the process? Those empty fields. Farmlands. Surely there would be food among farmlands?

He lay back and thought about it, thought
165 very hard.

John Christopher, The Guardians,
ELT Bd. 19. Penguin 1984, pp. 40–44
© C.S. & J.V.Youd t/a John Christopher

Annotations:

l.1 stint of penal labour – (hier:) Strafarbeit; ll.3/4 in the vicinity – near; l.4 stacking – piling up aufschichten; l.4 the House – the pupils of this boarding school (Internat) live in different houses; l.7 Prefect – senior … pupil given responsibility for keeping order; l.10 utterly exhausted – completely tired; l.16 dormitory – sleeping room; l.18 the Routine – a ritual use of strength to frighten new boys in the boarding school; l.20 grace – Aufschub; l.21 D`Artagnan – one of the three musketeers; l.27 lumoglobe – very bright light; l.28 locker – cupboard; l.31 disgrace – Schande; l.49 germy – carrying diseases; l.52 dumb – stupid; insolence – if you are insulting (unverschämt); l.64 disgusting – awful; l.66 tormentor – somebody who teases (ärgern)/vexes (quälen)/causes pain or suffering; l.72 pinion – bind the arms; l.75 decency – Anständigkeit; l.85 wince – show mental or bodily pain (zusammenzucken); l.95 grit – keep the jaws tight together; l.100 jab – Nadelstich; l.121 bully – frighten somebody who is weaker (einschüchtern, tyrannisieren); l.126 conurbs – town areas; l.141 dodge – trick, fool; l.142 derelict – dilapidated (verfallen); l.153 concealment – hiding; l.153 teeming – full of people; l.159 County – the area outside the towns.

A. Comprehension/Summary

Step 1 Let's have a look at the text from John Christopher's novel *The Guardians*. Read the text at one go.

Step 2 You have now got a basic idea of what is going on in this part of the novel. Let's jog your memory for a few seconds. **Where** and **when** does the action take place and **who** are the main characters? Take a few notes on the following page.

Step 3 The next step to get a better understanding of the text is to split it into several units and to find a suitable **heading** for each part. Use your text marker again and write the **headings** down (page 59).

Step 4 **Headings** serve as a rough frame of the action, but that is not enough. What we need for a good summary is the collection of the most important events and ideas (**main action**). Therefore try to put flesh on the bones of the following skeleton.

Be careful
Take down only the most important events and thoughts. If you are in doubt, go back to the information on summary writing given in Text 1, page 8–9.

place _____

time _____

characters _____

main action

units of the text	headings	development of the main events/ideas
1	Rob's <u>penal labour</u>	– <u>picking up</u> loose stones (result?) · ...

2	....	– eight senior boys out on the Routine <u>awake</u> Rob
		
		– they provoke him in several ways
		
		   a. ....
		   b. ....
		   c. ....
		
		– Rob's reaction
		   a. ....
		   b. ....
		   c. ....

3	....	– they let a rubber hammer <u>tap</u> on Rob's forehead – (result?) ➡ ....
4	....	– Rob <u>thinks of</u> going away either to .... – Rob rejects all these <u>possibilities</u> – the only possible <u>solution</u> that remains ...

What you have done so far is simply work on the four basic elements of a literary text:

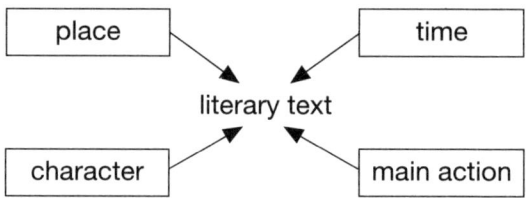

place → ← time
literary text
character → ← main action

Be careful
Please note that the main action might include important thoughts and ideas.

Step 5 Before you write out the summary, you should go on a fishing tour for similar words and phrases (= synonyms) as in a good summary you should **use your own words**. (See Text 1 again). There is one exception though, if some words are indispensable (unverzichtbar) for the understanding of the context or if they have been newly coined (= invented) as, for instance, the terms Routine, Conurbs or County in this story, do not change them.
So be creative. Rack your brain and find synonyms.

1. Underline difficult or important words.
2. Take your monolingual dictionary or any thesaurus.
3. Look them up and you will find useful explanations and synonyms.

In this case we have already underlined some of the words you should substitute in the skeleton.

You often find useful synonyms in the annotations. It might be helpful to look for appropriate generic terms (Sammelbegriffe), for possible enumerations of words such as 'domestic animals' for cows, pigs, ducks, etc.

There are three more things you should keep in mind before you start to write out the summary.

1. Remember to use indirect speech.

2. In order to further compress the sentences, the two most frequently used "tricks" are
   a. the shortening of relative clauses by reducing them to particular appositions
   b. the shortening of adverbial clauses by using infinitives, participles or gerunds.

3. Remember linking terms such as:

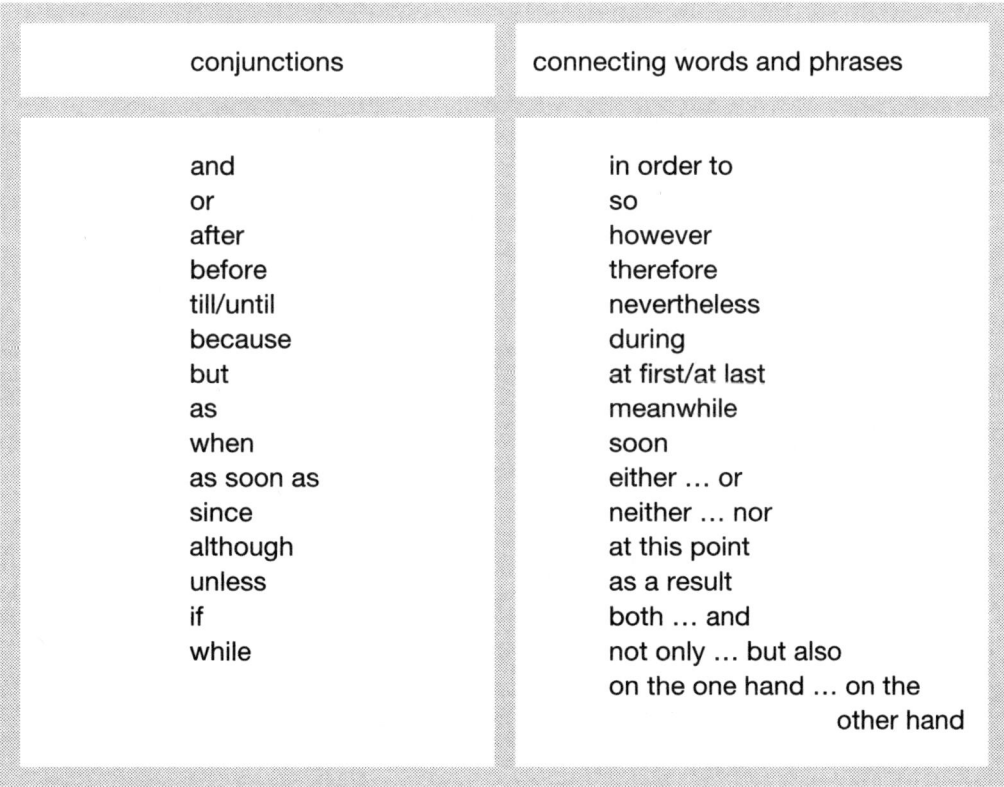

conjunctions	connecting words and phrases
and	in order to
or	so
after	however
before	therefore
till/until	nevertheless
because	during
but	at first/at last
as	meanwhile
when	soon
as soon as	either … or
since	neither … nor
although	at this point
unless	as a result
if	both … and
while	not only … but also
	on the one hand … on the other hand

Step 6   Now you are in an excellent position to fill in the gaps of the prepared summary on page 62.

Guided summary

After .... Rob Randall is awak-

ened .... They provoke him by ...., by

.... and by ....

Rob first decides to give in to .... and repeats what he is told,

but as he is not prepared to ...., they start to ....

.... After binding Rob they ....

Although the procedure is ...., Rob refrains from crying until he finally

....

This is the sign for his tormentors to withdraw. As a result of the ....

and with the prospect of .... Rob cannot sleep.

He therefore thinks about .... Since he has to reject

the possibilities of going to ...., of

...., or even of ....,

the only possible solution remains to ....

....

Step 7   Compare the following summaries the two 10th-graders Dagmar Siewert-
           sen and Sonja Pieck from Bad Godesberg near Bonn, wrote as test
           papers. Which one do you prefer? Say why.

Dagmar's summary

*After having done his first penal labour, picking up all loose stones near the house
and piling them up in a particular place one evening, Rob is very tired when he goes
to bed. As he is drifting into sleep, he hears the footsteps of the senior boys on the
Routine at the end of the sleeping room. Although there is a three weeks' grace for
new boys, the senior pupils come to Rob, too, with torches and lumoglobes in their
hands. Rob has to repeat the sentence that he is a disgrace and has to be ashamed of
himself, and he is told that he needs a House Punishment. The boys tell him to stand
up and to kiss their feet. But when Rob does not do that, they start to beat him with a
little hammer made out of hard rubber. Rob's head begins to hurt a lot, and after*

some time he starts to scream so that the boys stop beating. But they tell him that they are going to come back in the following night and go away. Because he can't fall asleep again Rob starts to think about what he can do. He knows that he can't go to his aunt, because it's too far, he can't go to the Kennealys, because they don't want him and he can't live on his own, because he hasn't got enough money. At the end of his thoughts he gets an idea: He could leave the Conurbs and go to the County and start to live there like his mother did before.

Sonja's summary

This night, the senior boys are out again on the Routine in the dormitory and this time Rob is going to be their victim. As he refuses to kiss the boys' feet, he is tortured. After a brutal lesson of manners and the senior boys' promise to return the next night, his aching head is filled with thoughts of escaping into the country where his mother had come from.

B. Comment/Composition

1. Would you like to go to a boarding school?

2. Do you think that Rob was right when he did not give in to the Senior boys?

Have you made up your mind as to which task you prefer? Okeydoke (= alles klar!). But hold on. Do not start to write your personal opinion straightaway. Remember the **essentials of comment writing**?

a) Introduce the theme of your personal comment by referring to the latest news on the radio, on TV, in the tabloids, magazines and newspapers; to recent debates or chat-shows on TV; to statistics or surveys; by quoting an expert or a scientist on the matter under discussion; by personal experience.

b) Structure your comment in at least three major parts
    – introduction
    – main part
    – conclusion

c) Write the main part by weighing the pros and cons of the topic and find one or two examples for each pro and con argument before you come up with your personal opinion on the matter.

d) Link the several parts of your comment by appropriate transitional phrases.

Topic: *Setting and Character in a Novel*   **Text 9**

Room with a Window.

A chair, a table, a lamp. Above, on the white ceiling, a relief
ornament in the shape of a wreath, and in the centre of it a blank space,
plastered over, like the place in a face where the eye has been taken
out. There must have been a chandelier, once. They've removed
5 anything you could tie a rope to.

A window, two white curtains. Under the window, a window seat
with a little cushion. When the window is partly open – it only opens
partly – the air can come in and make the curtains move. I can sit in
the chair, or on the window seat, hands folded, and watch this.
10 Sunlight comes in through the window too, and falls on the floor,
which is made of wood, in narrow strips, highly polished. I can smell
the polish. There's a rug on the floor, oval, of braided rags. This is the
kind of touch they like: folk art, archaic, made by women, in their
spare time, from things that have no further use. A return to traditional
15 values. Waste not want not. I am not being wasted. Why do I want?

On the wall above the chair, a picture, framed but with no glass: a
print of flowers, blue irises, watercolour. Flowers are still allowed.
Does each of us have the same print, the same chair, the same white
curtains, I wonder? Government issue?
20 Think of it as being in the army, said Aunt Lydia.

A bed. Single, mattress medium-hard, covered with a flocked
white spread. Nothing takes place in the bed but sleep; or no sleep.
I try not to think too much. Like other things now, thought must be
rationed. There's a lot that doesn't bear thinking about. Thinking can
25 hurt your chances, and I intend to last. I know why there is no glass,
in front of the water-colour picture of blue irises, and why the
window only opens partly and why the glass in it is shatterproof. It
isn't running away they're afraid of. We wouldn't get far. It's those
other escapes, the ones you can open in yourself, given a cutting edge.

From Margaret Atwood, The Handmaid's Tale. Virago 1987, p. 17 – 18,
published by Jonathan Cape.

Annotations:
l.1 relief ornament – Reliefschmuck; l.2 wreath – Kranz; l.3 plastered over – mit Gips verschmiert;
l.4 chandelier – Kronleuchter; l.12 rug of braided rags – Flickenteppich; l.13 archaic – very old; l.15
waste not want not – if you are not used to luxury you will not miss it; l.19 Government issue –
Regierungserlaß; l.22 flocked white spread – weiße Tagesdecke; l.27 shatterproof – bruchsicher;
l.29 given a cutting edge – if you have a sharp instrument.

A. Text Analysis

Info

Before starting to analyse the **setting of Atwood's text** we have to make sure of how to define **setting**.

To be more specific, the **setting of a narrative** is the general **place** and the historical **time** in which its action occurs. The place of the action can be further distinguished: it might refer to the **immediate environment** in which the events of a story take place (a room, a church, somewhere on a beach) or to the **general surroundings** (society, climate, standard of living, customs, values). The description of time and place is an important element in generating the **atmosphere** that surrounds the characters and the place of the action.

How to analyse the setting in a novel

Step 1 Now let's do a little warming-up exercise in order to grasp the basic elements of the setting. Take a closer look at the following pictures for one minute each:

© Y. Tempelmann

© Y. Tempelmann

Now imagine you find yourself in either of these two rooms. Tick off as many of the following adjectives as you think are suitable to describe the atmosphere you associate with the situation presented on the picture you have chosen.

Words

calm	dismal	reassuring
uneasy	off-putting	
peaceful	cheerless	dark
sober	tranquil	
spartanical	comfortable	sterile
cosy	pleasant	

Step 2 Now let's have a look at the **place**, to be more specific, at the **immediate surroundings** in Atwood's novel. Read the text once. Having done this take a pencil or text marker and highlight key words or key phrases that tell you about the immediate place of the action and the atmosphere there.

Example

A chair, a table, a lamp. Above, on the white ceiling, a relief ornament in
the shape of a wreath, and in the centre of it a blank space, plastered over,
like the place in a face where the eye has been taken out. There must have
been a chandelier, once. They've removed anything you could tie a rope to.

Step 3 Having done this pick out and list five to seven nouns and key phrases
that you think are important for the place of the action.

what we find in the text
_____

chair
table
lamp

white ceiling — relief ornament in the shape of a wreath

in the centre of it a blank space, plastered over, like the place
in a face where the eye has been taken out

there must have been a chandelier once

window ——— ....

....

floor   ....

picture ——— ....

....

....

bed   ....

....

Step 4 Having stated the evidence from the text, it's now time for you to use your
imagination, to rack your brain once again.
Try to draw conclusions from the examples you have compiled.
What kind of atmosphere is evoked?
Write your ideas next to the items above.

Be careful

When trying to find out about atmosphere – and that is interpreting the items you listed, pay special attention to **metaphorical language** the author has used to capture the atmosphere most effectively.

Decide whether such stylistic means are of any significance. Compare the use of metaphorical language in ll. 2, 3–4, 22 or the frequent use of the colour 'white' in ll.1, 6, 18, 22? And why are there blue irises (ll.17, 26) on the picture? Any idea?

what we find in the text	what we can infer
chair, table, lamp	barely/hardly furnished room
white ceiling ———— wreath	coldness, aura of death, decay, end of life; plus: glory or joy, as a wreath consists of flowers or leaves woven in a circle, worn on the head as a garland or placed on a coffin
...like the place in a face where the eye has been taken out	injury, violence, harm
chandelier	old building
window — opens only partly	....
shatterproof glass	....
floor —— wooden, highly polished	....
picture — framed with no glass	....
blue irises	....
bed — single mattress	....
sleep or no sleep	....
white spread	....

Step 5   What needs to be done now is to make sentences from the notes, but you can't do this without knowing a few linking terms. Therefore study the following list of terms:

Words

The | story | leads the reader into the world of …
     | action | is set in …
              | takes place in a (… confined area …)

There are various | hints   to suggest that …
                    | clues

The author gives a | rough   description of a room
                 | detailed
                 | vivid
                 | impressive

The author | describes   the room with | attention to detail
          | portrays | realism
          | characterizes

The description | presents many details of observation
                 | contains

The author | gives visual impressions of …
          | uses several words in a | figurative sense
          | employs | literal
          | underscores
          | underlines

The word in l. … | suggests that …
               | implies …
               | conveys the idea of …
               | evokes the image of …
               | conjures up the impression of …
               | calls forth …

What | is striking here is …
       | strikes me as … is …
       | reminds me of …
       | makes me associate …
       | makes me think of …

A striking detail	is, for example, …
The fact that …	suggests that …
The example of …	hints at the fact that …
	can be understood as

Furthermore there is …
Moreover
Another feature is …
This feature becomes obvious when …
Last but not least …
Finally …

So, all in all, we can conclude …
All things considered …
There is | proof   enough to say that …
         | evidence

Step 6   In the following paragraph on place and atmosphere you will notice **gaps**.
It is your task to **fill these gaps** with **linking terms/phrases**. If you are
unsure because several options are possible, check the list above.
When you have completed the task, try to memorize 10 expressions
starting with the one you like best or find most useful.

The action ……………………… in a prison-like room. There are various hints to suggest
this. From the start the author ……………………… a hardly furnished room, which only
seems to contain the bare necessities of life: a chair, a table, a lamp. The lamp, however,
suggesting light ……………………… that the portrayal is not meant to be exclusively
negative. A striking detail of the room surely is its white ceiling on which a "relief
ornament in the shape of a wreath" (ll.1–2) can be detected. The whiteness of the ceiling
……………………… the idea of coldness, of sterility, of being in a cellar or in an official
building, perhaps even of death. The latter idea is clearly ……………………… in
connection with the wreath-shaped ornament, as a wreath consists of flowers or leaves
twisted together in a circle placed on a coffin or – and here we have another positive
example – worn on the head as a garland.

Although ambiguous, the atmosphere of the room is predominantly ....

negative connotations. This .... when the author mentions

the window which 'only opens partly' (l.7–8) This is a clear sign that the inmates of the

building are not allowed out, if not forcefully confined within certain surroundings. The

picture with no glass is .... the authorities' precautions to

prevent the inmates from committing suicide. A third mainly negative association

.... by the mention of the bed, which is covered with a flocked white

spread. This image clearly .... a shroud. The fact that nothing takes

place in the bed except sleep or no sleep further .... an unusual

situation marked by a strangely relaxed inactivity or by pent-up sleeplessness. Last but

not least, the highly polished floor .... of a hospital again.

So, all in all, ... that the place of the action might be located

in a hospital for psychic diseases. The atmosphere .... forebodings of

death although it cannot be denied that there is a positive element to be noted all

through the text, which is given by the sunlight and by the blue irises.

Be careful
Notice that you can either put your main idea at the beginning of
the paragraph and then prove this thesis by the evidence you
have collected or leave the reader in suspense and come up with
your main idea at the very end of the paragraph.
In any case it is advisable to keep the best argument(s) for the
end.
When you structure your paragraph, you may of course change
the order of the list you made (cf. step 5) as it suits your argument.

How to analyse character in a novel

Step 1 Having analysed the atmosphere of the room, it's now very important to examine the **general surroundings** and to find out how the **character involved feels** about the room (and the society) he/she lives in. Therefore, go through the text again and mark the personal pronouns 'I' and 'they'. Underline the sentences referring to these pronouns. Having accomplished this task, proceed in a similar way as in Step 3 when you take notes.

I	they
can sit in a chair	have removed rope
can smell the polish	like a return to traditional values
am not being wasted	still allow flowers
....	....
....	....
....	....
....	....
....	....
....	....
....	....
....	....

Step 2   Now interpret the evidence you have collected. Put **your ideas** in the empty box next to the collection of examples from the text. Then continue.

I		they	
example	implication	example	implication
can sit in the chair	....	have removed	....
can smell the polish	....	like return to tradit. values	....
am not being wasted	....	still allow flowers	....
....	....	....	....

Step 3   What remains to be done now is to use the material you have compiled in Steps 2, 3 and write two paragraphs on the person's personal involvement in this society and about the political system he/she lives in.

B. Comment/Composition

1. You may have noticed that there are no clear references as to the time of the action in this extract. Nevertheless decide when the action takes place: in the presence, in the past or in the future? Give reasons for your choice.

2. Finally think about the function of the setting. Take into account that this extract is only the third page of Margaret Atwood's novel *The Handmaid's Tale*.

Topic: *Character in a Drama*   **Text 10**

Terry

Kids are waiting for a teacher. TERRY is sitting at the back, leaning back on his chair, looking out of window. The TEACHER enters.
TEACHER: Mornin'.
GIRL 1: Hia, sir.
5 BOY 1: All right, sir.
GIRL 1: All 'ey ... we're not doin' any work, are we, sir?
BOY 1: There's no point.
KATHY: We're leavin' next week.
TEACHER: Have you got a job yet, Kath?
10 KATHY: Yes, sir. Our Maureen's got me fixed up at her place y' know, Clifford's Biscuits.
TEACHER: Good, good. What will you be doing?
[During the following dialogue TERRY becomes bored. He takes out his transistor lead and surreptitiously plugs it in]
TEACHER: *[Turns to TERRY]* Terry ... what about you?
15 *[TERRY is unaware that he is being addressed. We hear music again]*
TEACHER: Have you got a job, Terry?
[TERRY stares at him but makes no effort to answer. The TEACHER is puzzled]
TEACHER: Terry ... Terry!
[The kids in the class turn and look at him and laugh. BRIAN, leaning across, unseen by TERRY,
20 *pulls the lead from his ear. TERRY is startled, sheepish]*
TEACHER: *[to class]* All right, all right ... Calm down ...
KATHY: He's always listenin' to that radio, sir.
TEACHER: Well, what are you going to do, Terry?
TERRY: Sir, I'll have a proper job, somethin' dead smart that I enjoy doin'. I'm gettin' a job
25 with travel prospects an' a car. An' when I grow up I'll have a wife who's dead smart with
proper, nice kids an' a house in the country an', y' know ... all that!
BOY 1: The only house you'll see in the country is the looney house.
[Laughter]
TERRY: You're the one who should be in a looney house. ...
30 TEACHER: Ah ah ah ... Now! Terry ... listen, how do you plan to achieve all this?
TERRY: What d' y' mean, sir? It just comes to y', doesn't it?
BRIAN: But y' have to work for it, soft lad.
TERRY: Well. ... I'm gonna work. But I'm not takin' the sort of job you've got, Lino. I'm not
clockin' in for the rest of me life. ...
35 BRIAN: Shut it, you ... soft. ...
TEACHER: Terry! Exactly what sort of job do you have in mind for yourself?
TERRY: Sir, somethin' in the music business.
TEACHER: The music business?
BRIAN: Sir, don't believe him, he's lyin'.
40 BOY 1: He's a looney, sir.

KATHY: Sir, he's not got a job in the music business. He's soft.

TEACHER: Terry? Well?

TERRY: Well, what. ... I'm not talkin' to them, they're just jealous.

TEACHER: Well, Terry. You've got to admit that this future you've got mapped out ... it does
45 seem a bit impressive. I mean the music business isn't one you just walk into, is it?

TERRY: No.

BRIAN: See. ... Don't believe him, sir. ...

TERRY: [*Pause*] But I know someone who's gonna get me fixed up.

KIDS: Who? Who is it ...? What's his name?
50 TERRY: Never you mind.

KIDS: [*Derision*] Ah. ...

TERRY: Sir ... I know someone in the music business. ... He's a good friend ... a really good friend.

BRIAN: What's his name?
55 TERRY: He's great, sir. Sir, I listen to him cos, cos the things he tells me about, y' know, about, like livin', they're the best things I've ever heard. ...

TEACHER: Well, I'm glad you've been listenin' to someone, because in the five years you've been in this school I don't think you've listened to any of the staff, have you?

TERRY: No, sir.
60 TEACHER: Well Terry ... all this good living that you're telling us about ... you'd stand a much better chance of achievin' it if you had listened to us.

TERRY: But, sir, all you and the other teachers, all you ever told us to do was study, an' work hard an' try our best an' take what we get. An' like sometimes I've tried to do that ...

KATHY: He's never tried to work hard, sir. ...
65 TERRY: Yes I have ... I've tried. ... You don't know about it, but I have. ... An' it's no good, cos it's too hard. ... There's too much against y'. Like if I'd started doin' that when I first come to school, when I was a little kid, I'd be OK. But I didn't. An' it's too late now. I'll never get what I want by just studyin' an' workin' hard. It's just dead lucky for me that I've got a friend like Float.
70 KIDS: [*Stunned*] Who?

Terry: Float.

BRIAN: Float Jones?

TERRY: Yeh

[*The class shout protests, claiming that* TERRY *doesn't know him*]
75 TEACHER: [*Getting the class quiet*] Look ... who ...?

KATHY: Float Jones. ... He's a DJ, sir. ...

BOY 1: On the radio. ...

BOY 2: How could he know Float Jones, sir? He comes from a different world. ...

TEACHER: Do you know him, Terry?
80 TERRY: Sir, he's a good friend.

[*The* TEACHER *nods, knowing what* TERRY *means.* TERRY, *turning, looks out of the window*]

From Willy Russell, The Boy with the Transistor Radio.
© 1979 Willy Russell

Annotations:
l.10 got me fixed up at – hat mich untergebracht bei; l.12 lead – here: Kopfhörer; l.13 surreptitiously – secretly; l.20 sheepish – embarrassed; l.25 dead smart – (sl.) very smart; l.27 looney house – Irrenhaus; l.32 soft – stupid; l.34 clock in for – nach der Stechuhr arbeiten; l.39 lying – to lie, lügen; l.43 jealous – eifersüchtig, neidisch; l.44 map out sth. – plan; l.48 gonna get me fixed up – going to get me a nice job; l.51 derision – hämisch sprechend; l.55 cos – because; l.58 staff – the other teachers at that school; l. 70 stunned – astonished, shocked.

A. Text Analysis

Info

A **character** in a play is a person whose personality we get to know very quickly and who is usually meant to be interesting, unusual or striking in one way or the other. There are several ways the playwright might inform us about the **characteristic traits/ features** of his or her character.

Firstly, the dramatist might describe the character's **outward appearance** (clothes, face, body, voice, age, peculiarities) either in the stage directions or by other characters. Secondly, **other people** might give their opinion or judgement about the character. Sometimes it is more satisfying to study what the character says (**his ideas and thoughts, values and attitudes**) and the way he talks, **his speech** (choice of words, sentence structures, speech level). You might of course say that actions speak louder than words. Therefore the character's **behaviour** (actions, gestures, movements on stage) must be of great importance. In addition to this hints might be given about the character's **environment** (his upbringing, living conditions, social background) and about his **position/status/role** as an individual within a social group.

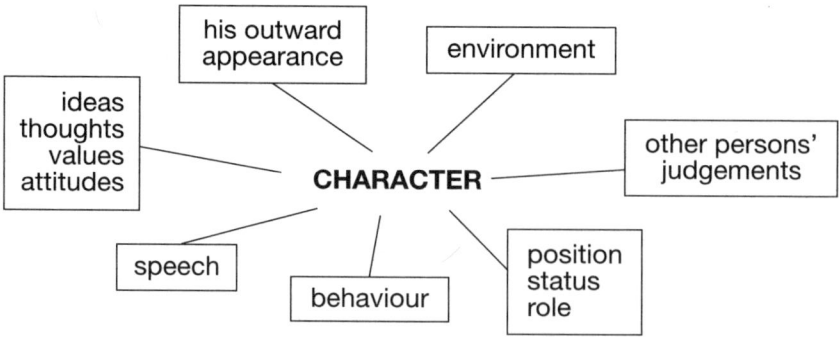

Be careful

As you will often have to analyse extracts of plays, it is obvious that not all the items mentioned above will be stressed equally by the playwright in this one scene. Let's see which of these categories become important in order to define Terry's character in William Russell's extract from his play *The Boy with the Transistor Radio*.

How to analyse character in a play

Step 1   First of all study the text carefully. If you are in class or among friends, why not try role reading, each of you taking a character's role. Do not forget to read the stage directions. There might be important hints as to the character's identity.

You will probably have noticed that the **other pupils** don't like Terry that much. Now take a text marker and underline or mark the passages where their dislike becomes obvious, where they openly criticise him. Notice who is against Terry and why.

Step 2   Having done this, write down five or six criticisms of Terry in the following way.

Example

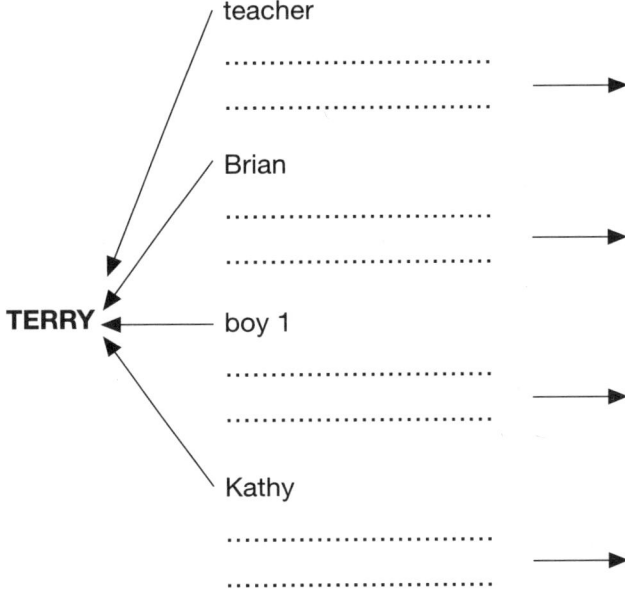

Step 3   You have probably guessed what follows next. Proceed by evaluating the
results of your investigation. Try to write down next to the five or six
examples you chose what we can conclude about Terry as he is seen by
his mates.
Perhaps one or two of the following terms might come in useful for your
notes.

Words

perfectly normal	odd/strange/peculiar
friendly/likeable	unfriendly/unpleasant/unlikeable
well-behaved	ill-mannered/uncivil
obedient	disobedient/unruly
attentive	inattentive/distracted
industrious/assiduous/diligent	lazy/indolent/listless
intelligent/shrewd	stupid/soft
quick-witted/sharp-witted	slow on the uptake/foolish/barmy
open/outgoing	reticent/uncommunicative
easy to get along with/	reserved/tight-lipped
sociable	
honest/ sincere	dishonest/insincere
quiet/calm	excited/full of beans
popular/well-liked	not liked

Step 4   You are now in a position to evaluate Terry's **position in class**, as you
don't need further examples from the text, perhaps with the exception of
line 1 (have a look again).
Close your eyes for a minute, then jot down what you think Terry's relationship with his classmates is.

Step 5   Having done this, write a paragraph on Terry's classmates' opinion of him.
Also refer to Terry's status in the class. Remember to start either by
presenting your conclusions first or by listing examples and presenting the
conclusion at the end.

Words

(Brian)	describes	(Terry) as …
	pictures	the characteristics of …
	portrays	the dominant features/traits of …
	characterizes	
	presents	
	points out	
	provides	

The relationship between… can be charaterized as

The description contains many details of …

these details	refer to …
	allude to …
	apply to …

This trait manifests itself when he …

Another feature is …
What is also striking about him is …
In addition to this …
Moreover …
Furthermore …

We might draw the conclusion that …

We	can infer that (Terry) …
	conclude that …

I suppose it is justified to say that …
Thus it is only too obvious that …

Summing up we might say that …

Taking everything into	consideration …
	account

To sum up

Step 6   We still haven't analysed Terry's **behaviour** and his **thoughts/ideas**, let alone his **speech**.
Let us get down to brass tacks (zur Sache!). Surely Terry's **behaviour** is unusual. The best thing is to use the same procedure as in Steps 3 and 4. Collect five examples that show the boy's extraordinary behaviour. Then try to conclude what these examples tell you about Terry's character.

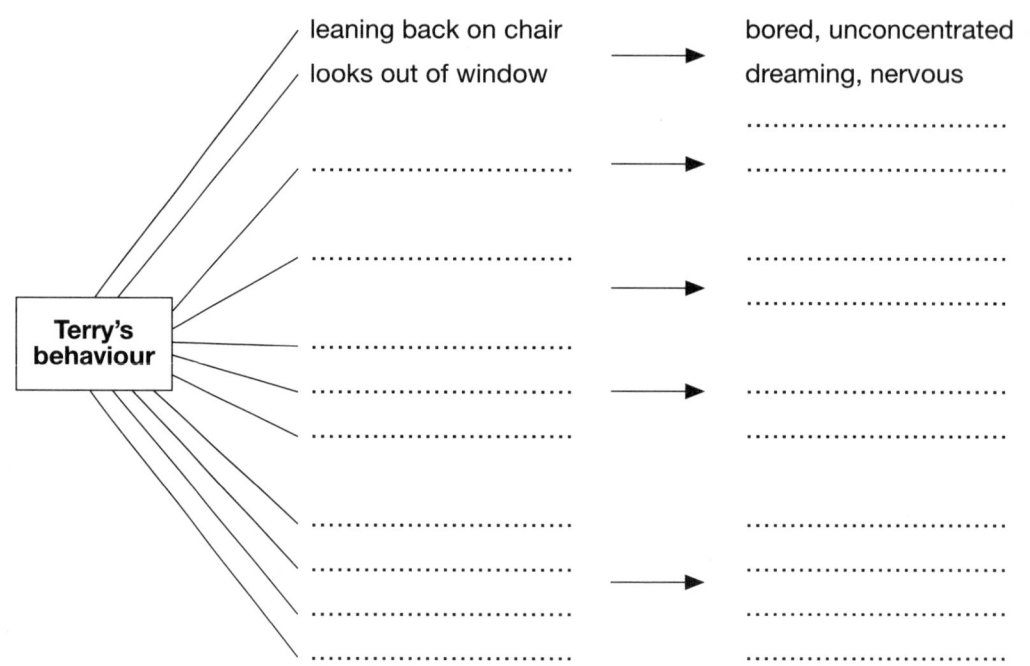

Write a paragraph on Terry's behaviour. Have a look at Step 5.

Step 7   Let's finally turn to Terry's plans for the future (**ideas and thoughts**). Once again go through the text with a differently coloured text marker, mark relevant passages and jot them down in the following way. Once again ask yourself what his plans for the future reveal about Terry's character.

Example

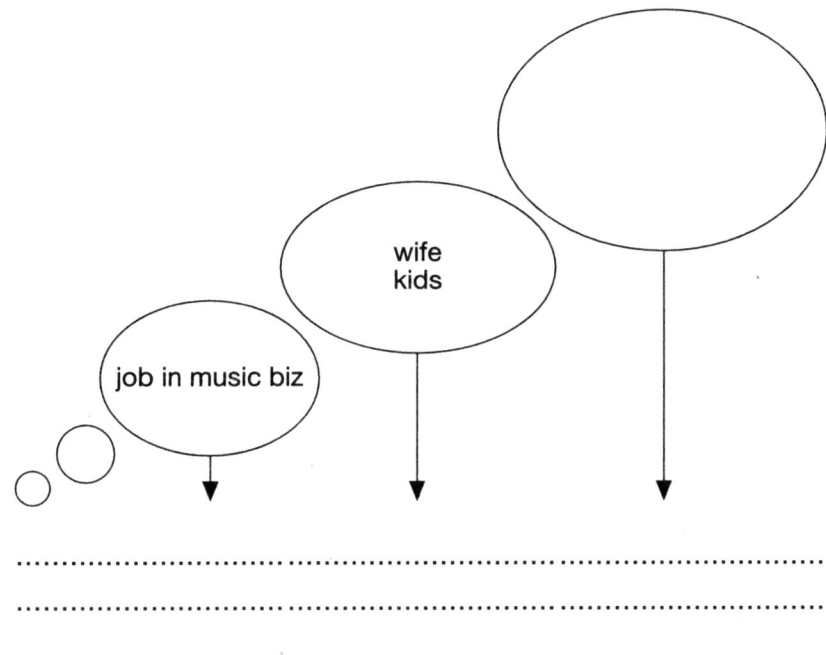

Step 8   To get an almost complete view of Terry's character, we still have to take a quick glance at Terry's **speech**. You have gone through the text so many times now that it will be easy for you to jot down four typical "Terry words". (If you need reminding, briefly skim through Terry's **ideas** and **thoughts** once again).

'Terryspeak'	corrected version
somethin' dead smart	....
....	....
....	....
....	....
....	....

What does this sort of language tell you about Terry's social background (environment)?

Take a few notes and have a break.

Step 9 What needs to be done now is to make sentences from your notes. You can easily build two paragraphs on ideas and thoughts and on speech.

Step 10 After all the hassle ("Zirkus") of taking notes and building paragraphs, lean back and read what 11th grader Susanne Bosch from Bad Godesberg near Bonn, wrote in a class test. List the various features of Terry's character that Susanne deals with (behandelt).

The excerpt "A Classroom" from "The Boy with the Transistor Radio" by Willy Russell is a scene of a play. It takes place in a classroom and comprises a dialogue between a teacher and his teenage pupils about having a job.
Terry, one of the kids, is a boy who is different from the others and who becomes the main person because of what he says. His outward appearance is not described. Terry is a dreamer. While the kids are waiting for the teacher, he is looking out of the window (I.2) and he does not even stop to do this when the teacher enters and the other pupils begin to have a conversation with him. His world of dreaming is music which is also about his only interest. When he hears music, he does not realize his surroundings. That becomes obvious in line 15: Terry is not aware of being addressed by his teacher, because he listens to music coming out of a transistor lead. As he is a dreamer, Terry does not think realistically, which is shown in lines 33 and 37. He thinks that you need not work to secure a good job, a car and a house of your own. And he is sure that he will become something in the music business. To conclude, he is very self-confident. He has a lot of illusions of his future, which can be seen in lines 24–26, when Terry talks about what he is going to possess. His dreams and illusions and perhaps his naivety give enough strength to him for feeling superior to the other kids and also to the teacher. He knows what he wants to reach in life and he does not intend to work hard (I.34). To convince the other pupils as well as the teacher of the fact that he will succeed in becoming a businessman in the world of music, he tells them the story of a well-known and admired DJ named Float Jones and argues that this man is a good friend of him who will support him (ll.48, 52/53, 68/69). Telling this story, Terry feels important and enjoys being admired by, for example, not telling the name of his "friend", although the kids ask him to do so (ll.50, 54). He describes Float Jones like a God and shows how much he admires him (ll.55/56) being proud to have such an ingenious friend.
Terry is not on good terms with the pupils of his class and with the teacher. He does not find it necessary to pay attention to the lessons and to the conversation between the teacher and the kids, because it does not touch his interests. So he clearly shows that he is not interested by looking out of the window (I.2), listening to music during the lesson (II.12/13) and giving no answer to the teacher's question (I.17).

Having started to discuss with the others, he feels misunderstood and makes clear that it is no use talking to them, because they don't want to listen as they are jealous (I.43). He does not like the other pupils as they do not believe him (I.29).

One important experience has determined Terry's way of life. When he started going to school some years ago, he did not work. And now it is too late to begin to work. He has tried it several times, but he has not succeeded. It is for this reason that he has decided to reach what he wants without working hard and studying (II.65–68). So the teacher accuses him of his behaviour to school and learning. He says that Terry would have had a much better chance of finding a job, if he had paid attention to the lessons (ll.60/61). The kids support their teacher in accusing Terry. They want to make Terry seem a stupid (I.22) liar (II.39, 74) and a lazy pupil (I.64) in front of the teacher. They themselves are of the opinion that Terry is very naive and stupid (II.32, 35, 41) and they do not conceal that from him. They make him out to be the clown of their class and only laugh about him (I.19).Terry stands outside of the community of his class. He is lonely, and so he thinks of a friend who is not his friend but who gives hope to him. That the friendship between Terry and Float Jones does not refer to reality, only becomes obvious in the end: "The teacher nods, knowing what Terry means."

B. Comment/Composition

1. Do you think Terry really knows the DJ Float Jones?

2. The teacher meets some of his colleagues later that morning in the staffroom. Tell the story he tells them of his lesson and his experiences with Terry.

3. Imagine that about 10 years after this incident Terry has become a famous pop star. One day he appears on a chat show ("Talkshow"). His old mates Brian, Kathy and Tom and his former teacher have also been invited. They have got a lot of questions to ask and Terry both remembers the old times, the problems he had at school, and his first steps into the new world of the music business.
Write the dialogues for this show.

Topic: *Character in a Novel* **Text 11**

Carmen Makes Her Entrance

[Having just entered the main hallway of Sternwood Place, private detective Philip Marlowe has a look at a picture when Carmen Sternwood makes her entrance.]

I was still staring at the hot black eyes when a door opened far back under the stairs. It wasn't the butler coming back. It was a girl.

She was twenty or so, small and delicately put together, but she looked durable. She wore pale blue slacks and they looked well on her. She walked as if she were floating. Her hair was a
5 fine tawny wave cut much shorter than the current fashion of pageboy tresses curled in at the bottom. Her eyes were slategray, and had almost no expression when they looked at me. She came over near me and smiled with her mouth and she had little sharp predatory teeth, as white as fresh orange pith and as shiny as porcelain. They glistened between her thin too taut lips. Her face lacked color and didn't look too healthy.

10 "Tall, aren't you?" she said.

"I didn't mean to be."

Her eyes rounded. She was puzzled. She was thinking. I could see, even on that short acquaintance, that thinking was always going to be a bother to her.

"Handsome too," she said. "And I bet you know it."

15 I grunted.

"What's your name?"

"Reilly," I said. "Doghouse Reilly."

"That's a funny name." She bit her lip and turned her head a little and looked at me along her eyes. Then she lowered her lashes until they almost cuddled her cheeks and slowly raised
20 them again, like a theater curtain. I was to get to know that trick. That was supposed to make me roll over on my back with all four paws in the air.

"Are you a prizefighter?" she asked, when I didn't.

"Not exactly. I'm a sleuth."

"A a " She tossed her head angrily, and the rich color of it glistened in the rather dim light
25 of the big hall. "You're making fun of me."

"Uh-uh."

"What?"

"Get on with you," I said. "You heard me."

"You didn't say anything. You're just a big tease." She put a thumb up and bit it. It was a
30 curiously shaped thumb, thin and narrow like an extra finger, with no curve in the first joint. She bit it and sucked it slowly, turning it around in her mouth like a baby with a comforter. "You're awfully tall," she said. Then she giggled with secret merriment. Then she turned her body slowly and lithely, without lifting her feet. Her hands dropped limp at her sides. She tilted herself towards me on her toes. She fell straight back into my arms. I had to catch her
35 or let her crack her head on the tessellated floor. I caught her under her arms and she went

rubber-legged on me instantly. I had to hold her close to hold her up. When her head was against my chest she screwed it around and giggled at me.

"You're cute," she giggled. "I'm cute too."

I didn't say anything.

Annotations:
l.4 delicate – soft, tender, fine; l.5 durable – likely to last for a long time; l.6 slacks – loose-fitting trousers as informal wear for women; l.7 tawny – brownish-yellow (lohfarben); l.9 tresses – hair; l.9 slate – kind of blue-grey stone that splits easily into thin flat layers (Schiefer); l.12 predatory – (of animals) preying upon others (räuberisch); l.13 pith – Kern; l.14 glisten – shine brightly, sparkle; l.14 taut – tighty stretched (straff; hier: schmal); l.22 grunt – make a low, rough sound expressing disagreement, boredom, irritation; l.33 sleuth – bloodhound, dog that follows a scent, here: (coll.) detective; l.40 tease – person who is fond of teasing others/making fun of others playfully or unkindly/annoying others; l.46 giggle – kichern; l.48 lithe – bending, twisting (geschmeidig); l.49 tilt – come into a sloping position (kippen); l.51 tessellated – formed of small, flat pieces of stone of various colour (mosaikartig); l.56 cute – sharp-witted, quick-thinking; attractive, charming.

A. Text Analysis

There is still one basic thing you should know when analysing characters in fiction. It is the distinction between **flat** and **round characters**.

Step 1   Study the differences between flat and round characters in the chart.

flat character ←→	round character
– merely a type/caricature	– complex
– constructed round a single quality (Eigenschaft)	– many-faceted (vielschichtig)
– presented without much individualizing detail	– characterized by a mixture of weaknesses and strengths
– undergoes little change	– may develop and undergo considerable changes
– can be described in a single phrase or sentence	– more difficult to describe

Step 2   Bearing this in mind read the text from Chandler's famous novel *The Big Sleep* and prove that Carmen Sternwood represents the typical man-eating vamp.

Step 3   Hold on. Do not start in a disorganised way. The best way to prove Carmen's flat character is by using the appropriate features for characterisation.

Do you still remember the seven basic features? Fill in the following chart.

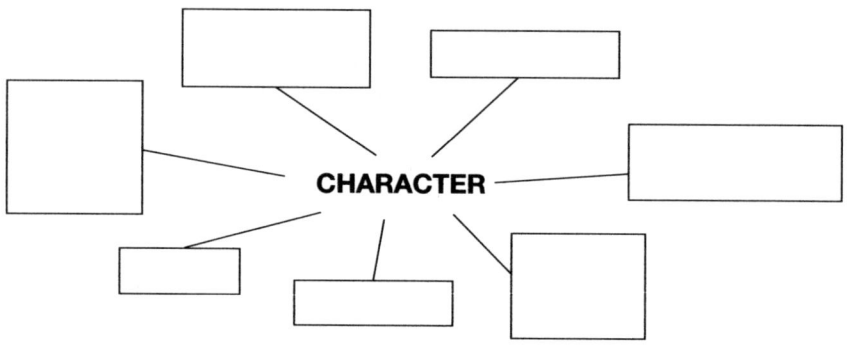

If you can't remember one or two items, check again on page 76.

Step 4   Well done. You are in good shape. Now gather some pieces of information on Carmen's **outward appearance** first, then proceed to **her behaviour** and finally notice **what Marlowe thinks of her**. Use the chart on page 87.

Do not forget to draw conclusions.

Step 5   By the way, lots of characters in fiction have got telling names which allude to or even sum up typical features of the person presented. The same goes for Carmen Sternwood.

You will have to check the name 'Carmen' in an encyclopedia. A mono-lingual dictionary will do for the adjectives 'stern' and 'wooden'. Put your findings in relation to this text. What can you infer?

traits/features	examples from text	what we can conclude
Carmen's out- ward appearance		
Carmen's behaviour		
what Marlowe thinks of her		

Step 6   You might guess that you still have to write a paragraph on Carmen, the beautiful blonde, the 'man-eater'. In order to give this paragraph coherence and structure , choose the most convincing four arguments (i.e. examples) and decide on an order of importance. Use the phrases on page 88 for your paragraph.

Words

Since Carmen Sternwood is | portrayed   as a mere type, …
                          | depicted
                          | described
                          | presented

She can be called a flat character. This is also the reason why she can be summed up in a single sentence: Carmen represents …

This extraordinary behaviour becomes most obvious in apparent ll.29–31 when she …

This gesture clearly suggests both … and …

In addition   to this the image of a woman sucking a thumb
Furthermore
Moreover

conjures up the idea of …
evokes

Another | significant | aspect   is Carmen's movement of the eyes.
        | important | detail
        | fact
        | example

Proof of this can be found in ll. …

This behaviour clearly indicates that …

Besides, the comparison with a theatre curtain hints at …

Finally Marlowe refers to this behaviour as a "trick" (l.20). This reveals that …

To sum up
All in all
To come to an end

Step 7   We will not let you go without having a quick glance at Marlowe who,
being the protagonist or main character in the novel, is of course a round
character.

Marlowe, it is true, does not say much in this short extract. Nevertheless
the few things he says, the way he views Carmen and the way he reacts to
Carmen's advances tells you a lot about his (round) character.

Trace examples in the text and draw conclusions as above.

	examples from text	conclusion
what Marlowe says to Carmen; his responses to her "passes"		
the way he views her		

Step 8   Write a paragraph on Marlowe as a round character using the arguments
from Step 7 and some phrases from Step 6.

B. Comment/Composition

1. How would you react if a girl whom you had never seen before
   addressed you in the way Carmen addresses Marlowe?

2. Later that day Carmen makes an entry in her diary referring to the
   encounter (Treffen) with Marlowe. Write the entry that Carmen
   makes.

Topic: *Setting, Character and Action in a Drama*   **Text 12**

Have You Noticed the Honeysuckle?

*A country house, with two chairs and a table laid for breakfast at the centre of the stage. These
will later be removed and the action will be focused on the scullery on the right and the study
on the left, both indicated with a minimum of scenery and props. A large well kept garden is
suggested at the back of the stage with flower beds, trimmed hedges, etc. The garden gate,*
5 *which cannot be seen by the audience, is off right.*

FLORA *and* EDWARD *are discovered sitting at the breakfast table.*
EDWARD *is reading the paper.*
FLORA: Have you noticed the honeysuckle this morning?
EDWARD: The what?
10 FLORA: The honeysuckle.
EDWARD: Honeysuckle? Where?
FLORA: By the back gate, Edward.
EDWARD: Is that honeysuckle? I thought it was … convolvulus, or something.
FLORA: But you know it's honeysuckle.
15 EDWARD: I tell you I thought it was convolvulus.
[*Pause.*]
FLORA: It's in wonderful flower.
EDWARD: I must look.
FLORA: The whole garden's in flower this morning. The clematis. The convolvulus.
20 Everything. I was out at seven. I stood by the pool.
EDWARD: Did you say that the convolvulus was in flower?
FLORA: Yes.
EDWARD: But good God, you just denied there was any.
FLORA: I was talking about the honeysuckle.
25 EDWARD: About the what?
FLORA[*calmly*]: Edward – you know that shrub outside the toolshed …
EDWARD: Yes, yes.
FLORA: That's convolvulus.
EDWARD: That?
30 FLORA: Yes.
EDWARD: Oh.
[*Pause.*]
I thought it was japonica.
FLORA: Oh, good Lord no.
35 EDWARD: Pass the teapot, please.
Pause. She pours tea for him.
I don't see why I should be expected to distinguish between these plants. It's not my job.
FLORA: You know perfectly well what grows in your garden.
EDWARD: Quite the contrary. It is clear that I don't.
40 [*Pause.*]

FLORA [*rising*]: I was up at seven. I stood by the pool. The peace. And everything in flower. The sun was up. You should work in the garden this morning. We could put up the canopy.

EDWARD: The canopy? What for?

FLORA: To shade you from the sun.

45 EDWARD: Is there a breeze?

FLORA: A light one.

EDWARD: It's very treacherous weather, you know.

[*Pause.*]

FLORA: Do you know what today is?

50 EDWARD: Saturday.

FLORA: It's the longest day of the year.

EDWARD: Really?

FLORA: It's the height of summer today.

EDWARD: Cover the marmalade.

55 FLORA: What?

EDWARD: Cover the pot. There's a wasp. [*He puts the paper down on the table.*] Don't move. Keep still. What are you doing?

FLORA: Covering the pot.

EDWARD: Don't move. Leave it. Keep still.

60 [*Pause.*]

Give me the 'Telegraph'.

FLORA: Don't hit it. It'll bite.

EDWARD: Bite? What do you mean, bite? Keep still.

[*Pause.*]

65 It's landing.

FLORA: It's going in the pot.

EDWARD: Give me the lid.

FLORA: It's in.

EDWARD: Give me the lid.

70 FLORA: I'll do it.

EDWARD: Give it to me! Now … Slowly …

FLORA: What are you doing?

EDWARD: Be quiet. Slowly … carefully … on … the … pot! Ha-ha-ha. Very good.

He sits on a chair to the right of the table.

75 FLORA: Now he's in the marmalade.

EDWARD: Precisely.

Pause. She sits on a chair to the left of the table and reads the 'Telegraph'.

From Harold Pinter, A Slight Ache and other Plays. Methuen Ldn. 1966, pp. 9-11.
Copyright by Faber and Faber Ltd.

Annotations:

l.2 focused – centred; scullery – Spülküche; l.3 props – stage properties – articles used on stage; l.4 trimmed – neat and tidy, in good order; l.8 honeysuckle – Geißblatt; l.13 convolvulus – Winde; l.26 shrub – a low bush; l.33 japonica – a type of ornamental bush; l.43 canopy – a hanging cover fixed above a seat (Überdachung); l.45 breeze – light wind; l.47 treacherous – false, deceptive (heimtückisch, trügerisch); l.56 wasp – flying insect with a powerful sting in the tail; l.61 Telegraph – The Daily Telegraph – a British conservative newspaper; l.67 lid – cover.

A. Text Analysis

How to analyse character and setting in a play

Tools ready? Let's go for **characterization and setting**. See how you like this dessert (Nachtisch) to the main dishes (Hauptgerichte) served in Texts 9, 10 and 11.

Step 1   Read the beginning of Harold Pinter's *A Slight Ache*. If your friends are around, why not share the fun of role reading?

Step 2   In order to get rid of a possible "slight ache" as to the understanding of the text, check the **time** and the **place** of the **action** first. In a play the stage directions usually provide significant information. Jot down the results of your investigation in the chart below.

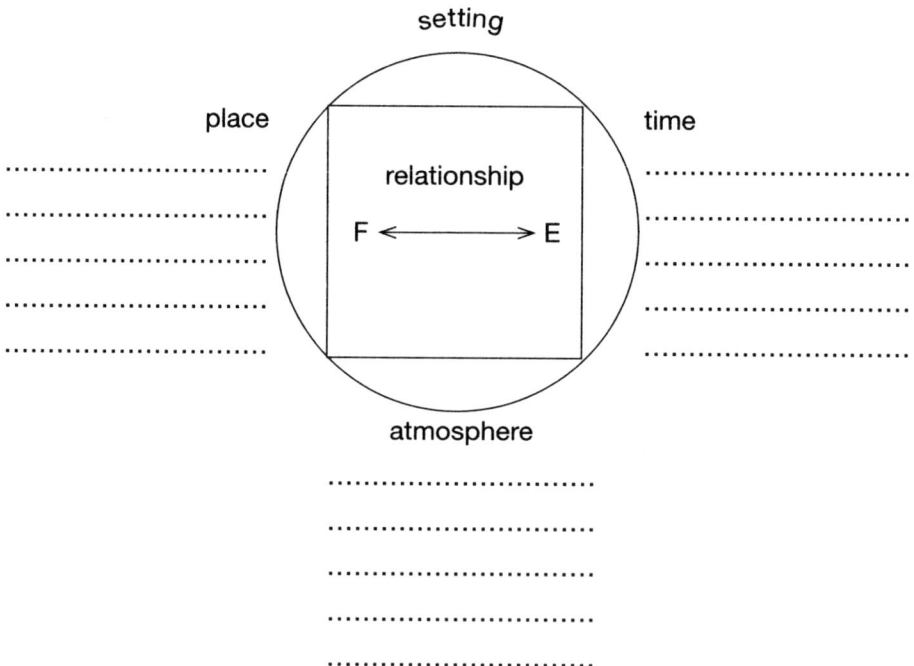

Step 3   What sort of **atmosphere** is evoked? Fill in your notes above.

Step 4   Now let's turn to Edward and Flora . At the beginning of the play (ll.1–53) it is Flora who seems to dominate the conversation. Try to prove her dominance by analysing the various conversational moves (sprachliche "Schachzüge") she uses in order to involve Edward. What is the impression you get of Flora?

Flora's conversational moves	F ➡ E		Edward's conversational moves
– question in order to start a conversation	Have you noticed?	Yes, yes. Oh	– monosyllabic answers ....
....	Edward you know that shrub	....	....
– reproach			

the impression you get of Flora

....

....

....

the impression you get of Edward

....

....

....

Step 5   How does Edward react? Pay particular attention to his use of language. What impression do you get of him? Employ the chart for your notes.

Step 6   Assess (=evaluate) Flora and Edward's relationship by choosing a score on the **marriage barometer** below. Briefly explain your choice.

What their relationship is like: the marriage barometer

+ 5	loving/affectionate/close/intimate
+ 4	full of respect/understanding
+ 3	attentive
+ 2	honest/sincere
+ 1	friendly/amicable
0	indifferent/disinterested
– 1	aloof/distant
– 2	dishonest/insincere
– 3	cold/burnt-out/benign neglect
– 4	disharmonious/quarrelsome/battling with each other
– 5	hateful/hostile

Step 7 With the appearance of the wasp, Flora and Edward's dealings with each other change dramatically. Trace this change in their speech. Find examples and draw conclusions. What other light is thrown on Edward's character? How does Flora behave in this situation?

Flora's conver-
sational moves

– confused
  responses

....

....

....

wasp

F   ◄   E

What?   Cover the
What are you   marmalade
doing?
                         ....
....
                         ....
....
                         ....

Edward's conver-
sational moves

– military order

....

....

....

Flora's character

....

....

....

Edward's character

....

....

....

Step 8 Now test their score on the marriage barometer. Same picture, any differences? See Step 6.

Step 9   Considering all this, has the setting changed as well? If so, take a few
notes. Does the setting mirror the relationship?

setting

wasp

place   time

relationship

F ⟵⟶ E

....

....

....

....

....

atmosphere

....

....

....

....

....

Step 10 Write a paragraph on the interrelation between relationship and setting in Pinter's first scene of *A Slight Ache*. Revise the terms in Text 9, Step 6 on page 69. In addition to this use the following phrases:

Words

In the first part of the introductory scene (l.53) the relationship between Edward and Flora can be | characterised as …
| considered as …
| regarded as …
| typified as …

They seem to | maintain   friendly relations with each other.
| entertain

Their | mutual   relations are …
| shared

They treat each other as …

The setting | mirrors …
| reflects

The atmosphere | is full of …
| heavy with …
| is tinged with …

How to analyse the structure of a play

Step 1 Lean back, relax a little and reflect on the way Pinter has started his play.

Any opening scene of a play serves several functions. For example it gives the reader an idea of the atmosphere. Can you think of other such **functions** of the **exposition**, which is the beginning of a play, in *A Slight Ache*?

Step 2 Now imagine you were the playwright and had to continue this play. Here is how it ends:

FLORA [*off*]: Barnabas
[*Pause. She enters.*]
Ah, Barnabas, everything is ready.
[*Pause.*]
I want to show you my garden, your garden. You must see my japonica, my convolvulus … my honeysuckle, my clematis.
[*Pause.*]
The summer is coming. I've put up your canopy for you. You can lunch in the garden, by the pool. I've polishes the whole house for you.
[*Pause.*]
Take my hand.

[*Pause. The matchseller goes over to her.*]

Yes. Oh, wait a moment.
[*Pause.*]
Edward. Here is your tray.

[*Pause. She crosses to* EDWARD *with the tray of matches, and puts it in his hands. Then she and the matchseller start to go out as the curtain falls slowly.*]

Well, what is happening here?

Step 3   Now invent some intermediate events of the action. Suggest how Flora
and Edward sort things out between themselves.
You might find some inspiration on how to proceed in the following graph.

Info
The action itself usually has a beginning, a middle and an end. The different parts of the
action have different names, which serve special functions.

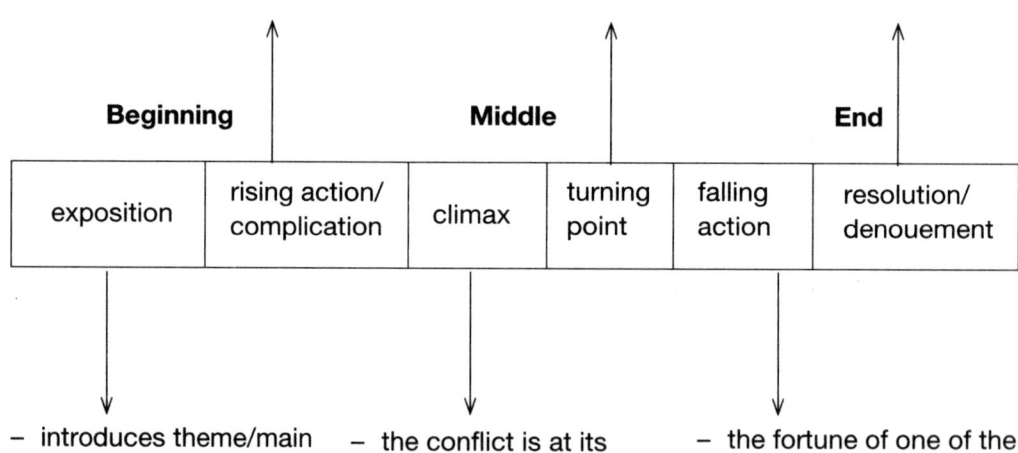

- a major change /crucial shift in the hero's fortune occurs /takes place

- reveals the fundamental error of the protagonist

- indicates the direction from which the resolution of the conflict is going to occur

- outcome of the conflict is decided

- action ends in success or failure for the protagonist

- shows the consequences of the hero's decision

- special incidents/events lead to a conflict

- increases the reader's suspense

Beginning		Middle		End	
exposition	rising action/ complication	climax	turning point	falling action	resolution/ denouement

- introduces theme/main characters/setting

- mentions important previous matters

- tries to awaken the reader's /the audience's interest/curiosity

- the conflict is at its most intense

- its resolution (Lösung) becomes inevitable (unvermeidlich)

- brings new stage of awareness (Bewußt-sein)/self-knowledge

- the fortune of one of the opposing forces drop lower and the other more and more controls the course of events

Be careful

Notice that there are of course other possible ways of arranging the course of events. So in some plays the climax is to be found at the end.

Read Pinter's ending once again and then let your mind work.

Step 4   In case you are interested in how the play really goes on, read the following text and underline the phrases referring to the different parts of the action.

Example

After the reader's interest is aroused by the appearance of the matchseller in the exposition, the rising action sets in.

Flora invites the matchseller into the house. In spite of Edward's desperate attempts to make the matchseller speak, the man does not utter a single word in the whole play. This and the fact that Flora, who seems to be sexually attracted to the stranger, tries to seduce him further increases the reader's suspense.

The climax is reached when the matchseller momentarily faints letting his tray fall. From this moment Edward's energy dwindles fast. The falling action begins. The turning point reveals Edward's fundamental error. He realizes that he has been living in a world of make-belief. The resolution of the conflict leaves Edward in a state of complete physical and mental exhaustion.

Barney

August 30th. We are alone on the island now. Barney and I. It was something of a jolt to have to sack Tayloe after all these years, but I had no alternative. The petty vandalisms I could have forgiven, but when he tried to poison Barney out of simple malice, he was standing in the way of scientific progress. That I cannot
5　condone.

I can only believe the attempt was made while under the influence of alcohol, it was so clumsy. The poison container was overturned and a trail of powder led to Barney's dish. Tayloe's defense was of the flimsiest. He denied it. Who else then?

September 2nd. I am taking a calmer view of the Tayloe affair. The monastic life
10　here must have become too much for him. That, and the abandonment of his precious guinea pigs. He insisted to the last that they were better suited than Barney to my experiments. They were more his speed, I'm afraid. He was an earnest and willing worker, but something of a clod, poor fellow.

At last I have complete freedom to carry on my work without the mute reproaches
15　of Tayloe. I can only ascribe his violent antagonism toward Barney to jealousy. And now that he has gone, how much happier Barney appears to be! I have given him complete run of the place, and what sport it is to observe how his newly awakened intellectual curiosity carries him about. After only two weeks of glutamic acid treatments, he has become interested in my library, dragging the
20　books from the shelves, and going over them page by page. I am certain he knows there is some knowledge to be gained from them had he but the key.

September 8th. For the past two days I have had to keep Barney confined and how he hates it. I am afraid that when my experiments are completed I shall have to do away with Barney. Ridiculous as it may sound there is still the possibility that
25　he might be able to communicate his intelligence to others of his kind. However small the chance may be, the risk is too great to ignore. Fortunately there is, in the basement, a vault built with the idea of keeping vermin out and it will serve equally well to keep Barney in.

September 9th. Apparently I have spoken too soon. This morning I let him out to
30　frisk around a bit before commencing a new series of tests. After a quick survey of the room he returned to his cage, sprang up on the door handle, removed the key with his teeth, and before I could stop him, he was out the window. By the time I reached the yard I spied him on the coping of the well, and I arrived on the spot only in time to hear the key splash into the water below.
35　I own I am somewhat embarrassed. It is the only key. The door is locked. Some valuable papers are in separate compartments inside the vault. Fortunately, although the well is over forty feet deep, there are only a few feet of water in the bottom, so the retrieving of the key does not present an insurmountable obstacle. But I must admit Barney has won the first round.

40 *September 10th.* I have had a rather shaking experience, and once more in a minor
clash with Barney I have come off second best. In this instance I will admit he
played the hero's role and may even have saved my life.
In order to facilitate my descent into the well I knotted a length of three-quarter-
inch rope at one-foot intervals to make a rude ladder. I reached the bottom easily
45 enough, but after only a few minutes of groping for the key, my flashlight gave
out and I returned to the surface. A few feet from the top I heard excited squeaks
from Barney, and upon obtaining ground level I observed that the rope was almost
completely severed. Apparently it had chafed against the edge of the masonry and
the little fellow perceiving my plight had been doing his utmost to warn me.
50 I have now replaced that section of rope and arranged some old sacking beneath
it to prevent a recurrence of the accident. I have replenished the batteries in my
flashlight and am now prepared for the final descent. These few moments I have
taken off to give myself a breathing spell and to bring my journal up to date.
Perhaps I should fix myself a sandwich as I may be down there longer than seems
55 likely at the moment.

September 11th. Poor Barney is dead an soon I shell be the same. He was a
wonderful ratt and life without him is knot worth livving. If anybody reeds this
please do not disturb anything on the island but leeve it like it is a shryn to Barney,
espechilly the old well. Do not look for my body as I will caste myself into the see.
60 You mite bring a couple of young ratts an leeve them as a living memorial to
Barney. Females no males. I sprayned my wrist is why this is written so bad. This
is my last will. Do what I say an don't come back or disturb anything after you
bring the young ratts like I said. Just females.

Goodby

*From Will Stanton, Barney. Fifty Short Science Fiction Tales ed. by Asimov and Conklin
1951, published by Fantasy House. © 1951 by Will Stanton*

Annotations:
l.2 jolt – jerk, sudden shake; l.2 sack – fire; l.2 petty – unimportant; l.4 malice – Boshaftigkeit; l.5
condone – forgive, approve of; l.8 of the flimsiest – weak; l.11 guinea pigs – Meerschweinchen;
l.13 clod – fool, stupid person; l.15 antagonism – opposition; l.19 glutamic acid treatment –
treated by a substance that in the 1950s was expected to increase children's intelligence if taken
as a kind of medicine (Glutaminsäure); l.22 confined – restricted; l.24 do away with – get rid of,
kill; l.27 vault – underground room (Gewölbe, Keller); l.30 frisk around – jump and run about
playfully; l.33 well – Brunnen; l.38 retrieving – finding; l.38 insurmountable obstacle –
unüberwindliches Hindernis; l.45 groping – trying to find; l.48 severed – cut up into two parts; l.53
chafe – rub; l.48 masonry – stones; l.54 plight – Notlage; l.53 breathing spell – Atempause; l.61
females – Weibchen; l.61 sprain – injure a joint in the wrist by twisting violently (verstauchen)

A. Comprehension

Does the story leave you somehow puzzled? If so, you are invited on a guided tour through the Barney maze Irrgarten). Try to answer the comprehension questions as quickly and as briefly as possible.

1. Where and when does the action take place?

2. What do the narrator and Tayloe have in common?

3. Who is Barney?

4. Repeat the narrator's reproaches towards Tayloe.

5. How does the narrator characterize Tayloe?

6. What is unusual about Barney's behaviour?

7. How does the narrator react to Barney's surprising behaviour?

8. The ending of the story is somehow weird (unheimlich), isn't it?
   If you still haven't noticed anything peculiar, compare the last entry of the diary with the preceding entries. What is different and what might be the reason for this?

9. Number 9 is only for those of you who are a bit slow on the uptake.
   So if you do not feel addressed, proceed to number 10. If you still haven't caught on (wenn der Groschen nicht gefallen ist), ask yourself who wrote the final entry.

10. Are there any clues in the entries from August 30th to September 10th that Barney is up to no good?

B. Text Analysis

How to analyse character and plot

Step 1   Since you are well-equipped with literary tools now, open your tool-box and produce the ones for characterising relationships (cf. Text 12). In this story we have a very peculiar relationship to work on. But before applying these tools we need some others. Do you remember? Yes, a "mini-characterization" of each character is on the agenda first.

    Since we have a **diary** in front of us, there is a fair chance to get first-hand information straight from the scientist's mind. Go and get it!

scientist	examples/evidence from text	your conclusions
what he thinks about Tayloe		
what he thinks about Barney		
his plans		

If you draw a conclusion as to the scientist's character, you may compare his ideas/ thoughts/judgements with your own perception of Tayloe and Barney.

Step 2   Point out two or three examples of irony that the author pours on the scientist. If you are not quite sure what irony is, read the following definition first:

Irony is when somebody makes a statement that is to be **understood in the opposite way**. If you say, for instance, that the weather is so nice but in fact it's pouring (regnet in Strömen), your statement is **ironic**.

Step 3   Go back to Text 11 to make sure what flat and round characters are. Then decide if the scientist is a flat or round character.

Step 4   Time has come to evaluate the relationship between the scientist and Barney. If you still hesitate, trace several stages in the "power game" between the scientist and Barney first. Who decides? Who has the upper hand? You might notice a change.

Step 5   The relationship between two **characters** is obviously closely linked with the causal construction of **action, setting, theme** and **central conflict**, which is called **plot**.

Is the tool box still open? If so, go for the different stages of the **action** and their **function**. Try to fill in the graph without cheating (by going back to page 98).

....	....	outcome of the conflict is decided
....	....	
....	....	....
....	....	....

Beginning			**Middle**			**End**	
			climax				

....	conflict at its most intense	....
....		....
....	....	....
....	....	....

Step 6   Decide if the different parts of the action on page 104 are also to be found in 'Barney'. Notice that the table is only an ideal one. Some aspects might not always have been taken account of.

As to the **resolution**, the action surely ends in a catastrophe (the scientist's death). The experiment of the supposed protagonist utterly (völlig) fails. The consequences of the hero's decision are clearly shown: The scientist who wanted to manipulate genes, thereby playing God, is punished with the loss of his life for his ambition, his blindness and his ignorance. A lack of scientific responsibility necessarily leads to disaster on a grand scale: the monster takes over. To sum up, it becomes obvious that genetic engeneering proves far too dangerous.

How about the **climax**? Is there an obvious **turning-point**? And what about **exposition, rising action** and **falling action**?

Read the story again. Then jot down your answers in the chart below. Notes will do this time.

different parts of the action	how this applies to *Barney*
exposition	
rising action	
climax	
turning-point	
falling action	

Step 7   Try to draw a graph reflecting the development of the action.

Step 8 Write a few paragraphs on the development of the action.

Words

The exposition	describes explains introduces states mentions
The action	begins is set in motion by is sparked off by follows a clear pattern
The complication	sets in when develops rises to up to increases reaches a climax culminates in its peak a turning-point
Sudden Unexpected events Inevitable	advance quicken the complication of increase the action arouse suspense
The climax	is reached when arrives is identical to reveals
The falling action	unwinds slowly to a denouement ends in catastrophe is brought down to
The resolution	leaves (Barney in a state of...) comes when brings ends in is open-ended achieves a happy ending

C. Comment/Composition

1. What could be Tayloe's reaction when he hears about his former boss's sudden death? Make use of your knowledge about Tayloe.

2. Imagine you are a critical journalist investigating the Barney affair. Write a leader for a daily newspaper.

3. Write a personal comment on animal experiments.

Topic: *Point of View in a Short Story*   **Text 14**

• 1 •

The events I have the privilege of telling you about are still on my mind as if they happened yesterday. You, dear reader, will sympathise with young Colin, who is the hero of our most unusual story. I hereby promise to tell you everything of import. Of how our young man came to be arrested on that pitiful day that changed
5 his life forever and why, after that, things happened the way they did.
The moment you met Colin you could not help being impressed. He was the most extraordinary lad if there ever was one. Long and skinny for his age, he had that lean and hungry look about him. And, one thing, he was born to run. When you saw him cruise by, you were reminded of … well … a greyhound, so effortless was his stride,
10 so elegant were his movements. I understand his family has always produced good runners, if nothing else. And many a time, you will pardon the joke, dear reader, they did have to run … from the police.
But let me tell you how it all began …

Annotations:
l.7 lad – young man; l.7 skinny – thin, bony; l.7 lean – not fad; l.9 cruise – here: run easily; l.9 stride –
Laufschritt

• 2 •

As soon as I got to Borstal they made me a long-distance cross-country runner. I suppose they thought I was just the build for it because I was long and skinny for my age (and still am) and in any case I didn't mind it much, to tell you the truth, because running had always been made much of in our family, especially running away from the police. I've always been a good
5 runner, quick and with a big stride as well, the only trouble being that no matter how fast I run, and I did a very fair lick even though I do say so myself, it didn't stop me getting caught by the cops after the bakery job.

From Alan Sillitoe, The Loneliness of a Long-distance Runner.

Annotations:
l.1 Borstal – Jugendstraf- und Erziehungsanstalt; l.6 lick – Tempo, große Geschwindigkeit; l.7
cop – policeman; l.8 bakery job – 'Ding', Einbruch

A. Text Analysis

How to analyse point of view in a short story

In this chapter you will get to know something about the way a story is told. Usually the author creates a **narrator** who **tells the story**.

Step 1 Compare the two texts on page 108.

Did you notice that the narrators are completely different? In the first text the **narrator** and the **main character** are two different people whereas in the second text the narrator and the main character are one and the same person, Colin Smith.

It therefore follows that the narrator's perspective or angle (Blickwinkel) from which he tells the story, often referred to as **his point of view** (Erzähl-perspektive), must be different. Consequently the **reader** perceives (nimmt wahr) the events of a story differently.

Step 2 Let's investigate the narrator's point of view in the first text a little closer. You should do two things now: Go through the text once again and mark what the **narrator** "does". Then ask yourself how the reader reacts.

what the narrator "does"	how the reader reacts
– addresses the reader	– is flattered
– knows everything	–
–	–
–	–
–	–
–	–
–	–
–	–
–	–
–	–
–	–

Info

It is perhaps a fair comment to call this narrator **Mr Know-all**. He refers to the characters by name or calls them he/she/they. He has a godlike position and tells the story from an **unlimited point of view**. He knows absolutely everything that needs to be known about the events and the characters. He even has access (Zugang) to the characters' thoughts, feelings and motives. Mr Know-all is also called an **omniscient narrator**.

The effect of his point of view on the reader is obvious. You can study it in the following graph:

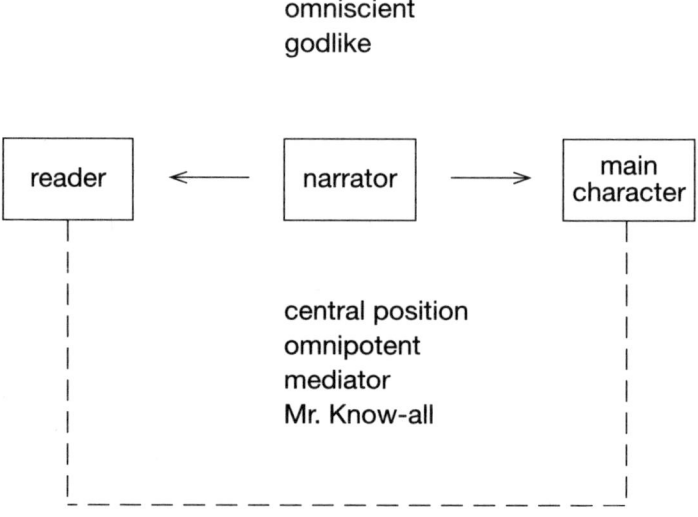

omniscient
godlike

| reader | ← | narrator | → | main character |

central position
omnipotent
mediator
Mr. Know-all

distance
detached relationship
indirect

Step 3 Let's examine the second text as to the narrator's purposes. Complete the table.

what the narrator "does"	what the narrator does **not** "do"	how the reader reacts
– gives facts	– plead for sympathy	– tends to believe narrator
– addresses the reader	–	–
– tells his own story/ reports truthfully	–	–
–	–	–
–	–	–
–	–	–
–	–	–
–	–	–
–	–	–
–	–	–
–	–	–

You can call such a narrator a **first-person narrator**. He is limited in his point of view to what he himself knows, experiences, concludes or finds out by talking to other characters.

What is the effect of the first-person narrator's **limited point of view** on the relationship reader/character? Fill in the graph.

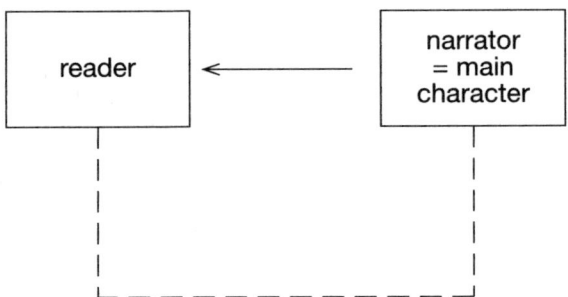

Step 4   Now read the following text. What kind of narrator has been at work here?

• 3 •

On 29th September Colin Smith, aged seventeen, was taken to a borstal in Nottinghamshire. He had been convicted of breaking into a bakery and stealing a considerable amount of money from the proprietor. His family background was strictly working-class. His father had been dead for a while when he engaged in criminal activities. Smith was particularly tall and
5 slender for his age, which, in the view of the director of the borstal, qualified him for running long distances. He improved his athletic skills and was nominated for the 'All England Borstal Cup' of the year.

Annotations:
l.2 convicted – verurteilt; l.4 proprietor – owner

Such a narrator is called an **absent** or **impersonal narrator** (= third person narrator). Try to describe what this type of narrator does and what he doesn't do. What is the effect on the relationship between the reader and the character? Again inscribe the graph.

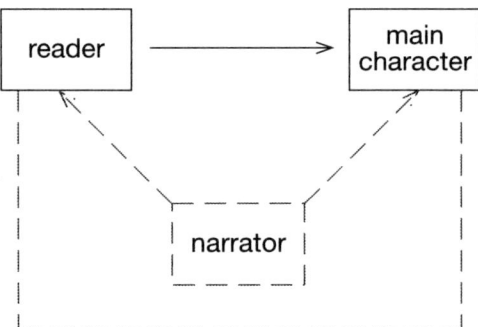

Step 5   You are in an excellent position now to judge the advantages and disadvantages of the three different points of view or methods of narration. Write them down in the chart on the next page.

Step 6   Are you ready for the last but one writing task? Well, here you go again. Compare the narrator's relation to the reader in two of the three texts of your choice.

	advantages	disadvantages
omniscient narrator (narrator knows the thoughts of all characters)		
first person narrator (main character, simply "tells" his/her own story)		
absent/impersonal narrator (narrator hides himself/ has no identity/only describes, reports, "shows")		

B. Comment/Composition

Borstals – a good "remedy" for juvenile delinquents, … and football hooligans?

Topic: *Imagery in Poems*   **Text 15**

At night, the moon, a pregnant woman,
Walks cautiously over the slippery heavens.

Richard Aldington

Above the quiet dock in midnight,
Tangled in the tall mast's corded height
Hangs the moon.
What seemed so far away
Is but a child's balloon, forgotten after play.

T. E. Hulme

The fog comes
on little cat feet

It sits looking
over harbour and city
on silent haunches
and then moves on.

Carl Sandburg

And the days are not full enough
And the nights are not full enough
And life slips by like a field mouse
Not shaking the grass.

Ezra Pound

Annotations:
haunches – part of the body round the hips (hier: Hinterbeine); tangled – verwickelt

A. Text Analysis

How to analyse imagery in a poem

You have successfully cleared quite a few hurdles on the way to an accurate interpretation of texts. One last challenge is yet to come though: how to crack ("knacken") images.

Let us therefore have a look at some of the poems from a group of poets called **the Imagists**. They were given this name because they believed that images are essential to poetry.

Info

The imagist poems on page 114 are short, atmospheric and basically built on the power of one **image**, with which they want to **challenge the reader's imagination**.

These poems are sometimes structured by first presenting an **Object A** and then comparing it with an **Image B**, which might also be further developed into **Image C**.

This means that an image is simply a comparison. For an image to work there must be some **similarity** or **point of comparison** between A and B/C. If the Image B is introduced by **as** or **like**, you call it a **simile**, if it is not introduced by as or like, you call it a **metaphor**. A metaphor is not always a noun. It can also be a verb, an adjective or adverb. A and B can also be people, ideas, qualities or animals.

Step 1   You have probably already spotted the Object A and the Image B, perhaps even the development of the Image B (= Image C).

What is the point of comparison? Sometimes the way to the point of comparison seems to be blocked. You might find that the key to enter it lies with checking the literal meaning of the Image B (in a monolingual dictionary) first and then thinking about its **figurative meaning** by way of association later.

Or to put it differently, you could ask yourself: What are the associations I have when I compare the literal meaning of B with the Object A?

Compare also Text 5 about denotations and connotations.

Step 2   Now off you go.
             Put the results of your findings into the following chart:

poet	object A	image B	image C	point of comparison
Aldington	moon	= a pregnant woman	–	round shape
Hulme				
Sandburg				
Pound				

Step 3   Give marks for each Image. Can you give reasons for your decision?

	very good	good	satisfactory	pass	unsatisfactory
Aldington					
Hulme					
Sandburg					
Pound					

The following adjectives might help you describe the images.

The image is	rather conventional	very original
	far fetched	highly suggestive
	rather obscure	effective
	hermetically closed	forceful
	extraordinary	daring
	surprising	dazzling
	stunning	breathtaking

Step 4   It's high time you wrote a paragraph on the image you have chosen as your personal favourite. Make sure that you mention the (two) elements of the comparison (A and B/C) and the three steps of discovering the point of comparison:

- the literal meaning of B
- your associations of B
- the poet's possible intention by using this image/ the effect the poet has achieved

Words

Make extensive use of the following phrases.

The poet	compares … with/to	
	draws a comparison between … and …	
	contrasts … to	
	connects … with the idea of …	
	associates	

The word …	is loaded with	connotations.
		implications.
	is connected with … in the poet's mind.	
	is associated with …	
	suggests	
	implies	
	conveys the idea of …	
	evokes	
	conjures up	
	stands for …	
	represents	
	symbolizes	
	refers to	
	is a symbol of	

Step 5 Now it's your turn to be inventive. Look at the items in the list below and find images for them. Choose at least three.

object A	image B	image C
anger came	like a mounting wave	swallowing kindness and communication
teachers are		
the sun		
Bonn at rush-hour		
school at 8 p.m.		
depression settled		
the caterpillar crawled		
frustration		
pent-up emotions		

When you have jotted down your images, read your short imagist poems to your boy-friend or girl-friend.

Step 6   Look at the following pictures to create your own developed imagist
poems.

Hannah Höch, Die Braut oder Pandorra, 1927; Berli-   © *Bucher-Verlag GmbH, München*
nische Galerie, Museum für Moderne Kunst, Photogra-
phie und Architektur. © *VG Bild-Kunst, Bonn 1994*

Step 7   Look again at Aldington and Hulme's poems and find a way of composing
similar poems for other celestial bodies (Himmelskörper).

Use the same pattern: Start with a mention of the time of day, add a more
detailed description of the action or effect of the celestial body on you and
finally come up with a striking image.

Glossar

abandon all hope that	alle Hoffnung aufgeben, daß
absent (narrator)	abwesender (Erzähler)
access to	Zugang zu
accomplish a task	eine Aufgabe erfüllen
accordingly	entsprechend
account for	erklären, erläutern
achieve s.th.	etwas erreichen
the action is set in	der Schauplatz der Handlung ist
the action is set in motion by	die Handlung wird ausgelöst durch
the action unwinds	die Handlung rollt ab
add	hinzufügen
address the reader by	den Leser ansprechen durch
adopt the point of view of	die Perspektives eines … einnehmen
advance s.th.	hier: vorantreiben
aim for the reader to	darauf zielen , daß der Leser …
alliance	hier: Zusammengehen
allude to s.th.	auf etwas anspielen
aloof	distanziert
ambiguous	mehrdeutig, ambivalent
ambition; ambitious	Ehrgeiz, Machthunger; ehrgeizig
another significant aspect is	ein weiterer bedeutender Aspekt ist
apparent	offensichtlich
antithetical	gegensätzlich
appealing	ansprechend
apply to	gelten für
apply tools to	Werkzeuge anwenden
appropriate	passend, geeignet
argument proper	das eigentliche Argument
arise from the fact that	aus der Tatsache hervorgehen, daß
arouse s.th.	etwas hervorrufen
assess s.th.as	etwas bewerten als
assiduous	fleißig, strebsam
the atmosphere is heavy with	die Atmosphäre ist geladen mit
atrocity	Grausamkeit, Scheußlichkeit
available to	verfügbar für
average reader	Durchschnittsleser
avoid (doing) s.th.	etwas (zu tun) vermeiden
baffled	verwirrt, ratlos
the bare necessities of life	die einfachsten Bedürfnisse des Lebens
barmy	dumm, bekloppt
bearing in mind that	wenn man sich vor Augen hält, daß
be aware of s.th.	sich einer Sache bewußt sein
be important to	wichtig sein für
be (not) prepared to do s.th.	(nicht) willens sein, etwas zu tun
be up to no good	nichts Gutes im Schilde führen
be well-advised (not) to	gut beraten sein, etwas (nicht) zu tun
benign neglect	laues Nebeneinanderherleben
broad range of vocabulary	große Spannweite im Vokabular
briefly explain	erläutere kurz
bring home one's point	erfolgreich argumentieren

browse through a text	einen Text durchblättern
by comparison	im Gegensatz dazu
can be read/understood as	kann interpretiert werden als
catalyst; catalytic (character)	jemand, an dem sich Gut und Böse scheiden
catch on	der Groschen fällt
captivating	fesselnd
capture s.th.	etwas einfangen
causal construction	kausale Verknüpfung
cause-to-effect	Ursache und Wirkung
challenge the reader's imagination	die Phantasie des Lesers herausfordern
chart	Tabelle
chat show	Diskussionssendung
cheerless	freudlos
choice of words	Wortwahl
closely linked with	eng verbunden mit
a closer look reveals that	eine genauerer Blick enthüllt, daß
clue	Hinweis, Indiz
clumsy	unbeholfen, schwerfällig
coherence; coherent	Zusammenhang; zusammenhängend
come full circle	sich vollkommen verändern
come to grips with	klarkommen mit
comes hardly as a surprise	ist kaum eine Überraschung
common core of English	Kernbereich des Englischen
a commonly held view is that	eine verbreitete Ansicht ist, daß
compelling	zwingend, überzeugend
compile s.th.	etwas zusammenstellen
the complication of the action	die Verwicklung der Handlung
compound clause	Satzgefüge
comprehension; comprehensible	Verständnis; verständlich
concern s.th.	etwas betreffen
conclusion; conclude s.th.	Schlußfolgerung; etwas schlußfolgern
confirm	bestätigen, untermauern
conjure up s.th.	etwas heraufbeschwören
connotation; connote s.th.	assoziative Bedeutung
consequently	folglich, infolgedessen
consistent	konsequent
conspicuous	auffallend, eindrucksvoll
continue with what can be called	fährt fort mit
convey s.th.	etwas vermitteln
convincing end	ein überzeugender Schluß
cope with	zurechtkommen mit
correspondences	Entsprechungen
counterargument	Gegenargument
counterpart	Gegenstück
course of events	der Ablauf der Ereignisse
crack an image	ein Bild knacken
credibility; credible	Glaubwürdigkeit; glaubwürdig
crucial shift	wesentliche Wendung
culminate in s.th.	in etwas gipfeln
curiosity aroused by	Neugier, erweckt durch
daft	doof, bekloppt, blöd
dangling participle clause	unverbundenes Partizip
dazzling	glänzend, schön

deal with	handeln von, sich befassen mit
deliberately	bewußt, gezielt
delighted	entzückt
denouement	Auflösung
denotation; denote s.th.	ursprüngliche, wörtliche Bedeutung
depict s.th.	etwas abbilden, beschreiben
dependent clause	Nebensatz
devote space to	einer Sache Platz einräumen
diary; diary entry	Tagebuch; Tagebucheintrag
diligent	strebsam, eifrig
discernible middle	klar erkennbarer Mittelteil
disclose s.th.	etwas enthüllen, aufdecken
disconcerting	beunruhigend
dismal	trübe, niederschmetternd
dispense with s.th.	verzichten auf etwas, auskommen ohne
disregard s.th.	etwas mißachten
distinction; distinguish from	Unterscheidung; unterscheiden von
distracted	abgelenkt, unaufmerksam
draw a conclusion	eine Schlußfolgerung ziehen
draw a parallel between	eine Parallele ziehen zwischen
due to	ist zurückzuführen auf
educated reader	gebildeter Leser
elicit key words	Schlüsselwörter heraussuchen
elliptic clause	unvollständiger Satz
emphasize s.th.	etwas betonen
employ	verwenden, gebrauchen
enlarge on	genauere Ausführungen machen zu
enumerate	aufzählen, aufreihen
s.th. is equivalent to	etwas entspricht, ist gleichzusetzen
establish thematic coherence by	thematische Geschlossenheit sichern durch
events (of a story)	Ereignisse einer Geschichte
eventually	schließlich, endlich
evidence	Belege, Beweismaterial
evaluate	bewerten
evoke an atmosphere	eine Atmosphäre heraufbeschwören
exhilarating	belustigend
exclude s.th.	etwas ausschließen
exposition	Einführung in Ort, Zeit, Figuren und Handlung
express one's relief at	seine Erleichterung ausdrücken über
falling action	fallende Handlung
far-fetched	weit hergeholt
favour s.th.	sich für etwas aussprechen
feature	Merkmal
feel strongly about	entschieden ablehnen
fidgety	zappelig, unruhig
figurative meaning	übertragene Bedeutung
first draft	erster Entwurf
first-person narrator	Ich-Erzähler
flat character	eindimensionaler Charakter, Typ
flick through a text	einen Text durchblättern
for one thing … for another	zum einen … zum anderen
for what purpose	zu welchem Zweck
frequently	häufig

fuel the reader's interest	des Lesers Interesse speisen
full of beans	zappelig
gap	Lücke
generic term	Sammelbegriff
get down to brass tacks	zur Sache kommen
get rid of s.th.	etwas loswerden
gist	Kernaussage
go down well with s.b.	gut ankommen bei
go into particulars	ins Detail gehen
go over the text	den Text durchgehen
grasp (the contents)	verstehen, kapieren
handling of the words	Umgang mit Wörtern
hassle	Zirkus
heading	Überschrift
hermetically closed	völlig unverständlich
highflying	ehrgeizig
highlight s.th.	etwas hervorheben, unterstreichen
hinge on s.th.	abhängen von, ankommen auf
hint at s.th.	etwas andeuten
I am in two minds about	ich kann mich nicht entscheiden
I can see the point, yet I wonder	ich kann das nachvollziehen, frage mich jedoch …
I fail to see why	ich kann den Grund nicht erkennen
I simply cannot believe that	ich kann einfach nicht glauben, daß
ignorance; ignorant	Unwissen; unwissend
ill-bred	schlecht erzogen
imagery	Bildlichkeit
immediate	unmittelbar
impact on s.th.	Auswirkung auf
impersonal (narrator)	unpersönlicher (Erzähler)
inconsistency; inconsistent	logischer Bruch, Ungereimtheit
include s.th.	etwas berücksichtigen
indicate	anzeigen, hinweisen auf
indifference; indifferent	Gleichgültigkeit; gleichgültig
indispensable	unverzichtbar
indolent	faul, träge
industrious	fleißig, strebsam
inevitable	unausweichlich
in fact one might say that	man kann in der Tat behaupten, daß
infer s.th.	schlußfolgern, ableiten
ingenious	vorzüglich, geistreich
in retrospect	in der Rückschau
intersperse a text with	einstreuen
in the first place	überhaupt erst
investigation; investigate s.th.	Untersuchung; etwas untersuchen
involved (the character)	betroffen
item	Beispiel, Einzelheit
it is difficult to classify	es ist schwierig einzuordnen
it is more than doubtful whether	es ist mehr als zweifelhaft, ob
it is often argued that	es wird oft argumentiert, daß
it is safe to say that	man darf wohl behaupten, daß
it stands to reason that	es leuchtet ein, daß
it therefore follows that	es folgt daher, daß

jar with	nicht passen zu
jot down s.th.	etwas niederschreiben, notieren
juxtapose disparate elements	nicht passende Elemente gegenüberstellen
lack of	Mangel an
last but not least	schließlich, letztendlich
leave the reader in suspense	den Leser unter Spannung halten
s.th. lends itself to	etwas eignet sich gut für
letter to the editor	Leserbrief
lexical choices	Wortwahl
likeable	sympathisch, nett
limited (point of view)	beschränkter (Erzählwinkel)
limit o.s. to	sich beschränken auf
line of thought	Gedankengang, Gedankenabfolge
linking terms	Gelenkvokabular
listing	aufzählend
listless	matt, teilnahmslos, apathisch
literal meaning	wörtliche Bedeutung
main clause	Hauptsatz
maintain a relationship	eine Beziehung unterhalten
to make things worse (for)	was die Dinge schlimmer macht (für)
many-faceted	vielschichtig
manifest	offenbar, sichtbar, deutlich
start medias-in-res	sofort loslegen
s.th. manifests itself in	etwas zeigt sich in
mediator	Vermittler
meet s.b. halfway	jemandem auf halbem Wege entgegenkommen
metaphor; metaphorical	impliziter Vergleich; metaphorisch; bildlich
mirror s.th.	etwas spiegeln
monosyllabic answers	einsilbige Antworten
more (most) importantly	was noch wichtiger ist, ...
mutual relations	wechselseitige Beziehungen
my explanation is that	meine Erklärung ist, daß
my own experience tells me that	meine eigene Erfahrung geht dahin, daß
mystifying	verwirrend
narrator; narrative	Erzähler; erzähl ...
nasty	unflätig, fies
newly coined	neu geprägt
news story	Zeitungsgeschichte
obedient	achtungsvoll
obscure	dunkel, unverständlich
occupy a position of	eine Position von ... einnehmen
occur	auftauchen
off-putting	abschreckend, ernüchternd
omit s.th.	etwas auslassen, nicht berücksichtigen
omnipotent	allmächtig
omniscient (narrator)	allwissender (Erzähler)
on the agenda	auf dem Programm
outgoing	gesellig, zugänglich
outward appearance	äußeres Erscheinungsbild
overall effect	Gesamteindruck
owing to	zurückzuführen auf

paragraph	Absatz
peak	Gipfel, Höhepunkt
peculiarities, peculiar	Besonderheiten; ungewöhnlich
pent-up	aufgestaut
pepper one's text with	seinen Text aufpeppen mit
perception of; perceive s.th.	Wahrnehmung von; etwas wahrnehmen
persuade s.b.	jemanden überreden
persuasive	beeinflussend
plead for sympathy	um Sympathie werben
point of view	Erzählperspektive
point to s.th.	auf etwas hindeuten
pointless (violence)	sinnlose (Gewalt)
predominant	vorherrschend
prefer s.th. over s.th else	einer Sache den Vorrang einräumen vor
prevail	vorherrschen
previous	vorausgehend
progressive	fortschreitend
proceed	vorgehen
proof of this can be found in	dies läßt sich belegen in
protagonist	Hauptfigur, Held
put flesh on the bones	etwas auffüllen, abrunden
put it differently	es anders ausdrücken
put s.th. down to the fact that	etwas zurückführen auf
provide an answer to	eine Antwort liefern für
provide information on	Informationen liefern zu
put forth a personal view	einen persönlichen Standpunkt vorbringen
put it in a nutshell	um es kurz zu machen
quarrelsome	streitsüchtig
quick-/sharp-witted	schlagfertig
quotations; quote	Zitate; zitieren
random selection	Zufallsauswahl
realm of summary writing	Feld (=Reich) des Summary-Schreibens
refer to; reference	sich beziehen auf; Bezug auf
reflect s.th.	etwas spiegeln
refrain from doing s.th.	sich etwas versagen
reinforce s.th.	etwas verstärken, untermauern
reticent	zurückhaltend, verschwiegen
reveal s.th.	etwas enthüllen
review s.th.	etwas wiederholen
recur	wiederkehren
respond to	reagieren auf
resolution	Auflösung
restrict o.s. to	sich beschränken auf
reversal of roles	Verkehrung der Rollen
rich in implications	reich an Anspielungen
rising action	steigende Handlung
round character	komplexe Figur, voll ausgestalteter Charakter
scan a text	einen Text absuchen nach
scarce	spärlich, selten
scattered over	verstreut über
score with	Punkte sammeln mit
seems hard/impossible to grasp	erscheint schwer/unmöglich zu durchschauen

sequence of	Abfolge von
serve as	dienen als
serve a function	eine Funktion erfüllen
setting	Ort/Zeit/Atmosphäre
serve s.b.'s purposes	jemandes Zwecken dienen
shrewd	scharfsinnig, schlau
significance	Gewicht, Bedeutung
similarity; similar to	Ähnlichkeit; ähnlich mit
simile	ausdrücklicher Vergleich
a situation marked by	eine Situation, gekennzeichnet durch
skeleton; skeleton layout	Gerüst, Skelett
skilfully chosen	geschickt gewählt
skim through a text	einen Text überfliegen
slant the text	den Text verfälschen
slot	Spalte
slow on the uptake	schwer von Begriff
snappy	forsch, schwungvoll
sober	nüchtern, unromantisch
sociable	gesellig
soft	dumm, beschränkt
sort s.th out	etwas ordnen, sortieren
sparked off by	ausgelöst durch
speech level	Sprachebene, Register
spot s.th.	etwas herausbekommen
stage direction	Bühnenanweisung
stage of awareness	Bewußtseinsstand
start off with	beginnen mit
state one's opinion	seine Meinung zum Ausdruck bringen
state the case for	die Position für … vertreten
stimulating	anregend
stick to	sich halten an
stir s.b.'s imagination	jemandes Phantasie anregen
strike a note	einen Ton anschlagen
striking	auffällig, ins Auge stechend
a striking example of	ein schlagendes Beispiel für
structural pattern	Strukturmuster
studied behaviour	einstudiertes Verhalten
stunning	phänomenal, atemberaubend
suggest	nahelegen
supports the idea that	unterstreicht die Idee, daß
suppress	hier: unterschlagen
surroundings	Milieu, soziales Umfeld
suitable	passend, geeignet
substitute s.th.	etwas ersetzen
survey	Umfrage, statistische Erhebung
sustain the reader's interest	des Lesers Interesse wachhalten
sweeping	kompromißlos, radikal
sympathy	Mitgefühl, Verständnis
synonym	Wort oder Ausdruck mit ähnlicher Bedeutung
syntax; syntactic choices	Satzbau
tabloid	Sensationsblatt
take a quick glance at	einen schnellen Blick werfen auf
take an interest in	sich interessieren für
take off forcefully	kraftvoll beginnen

taking everything into consideration/account	wenn man alles berücksichtigt
tamper with	hantieren mit, herumdoktern an
technical terms	Fachausdrücke
this is further enhanced because	das wird gesteigert, weil
tells a different story	läßt die Sache anders aussehen
temporal structure	zeitliche Reihenfolge
there is no denying that	es läßt sich nicht leugnen, daß
there is some evidence to suggest	es gibt Belege dafür, daß
thesaurus	Synonym-Wörterbuch
thrilled	erregt, gespannt
tinged with	durchtränkt von, getönt mit
topic; current topic	Thema; aktuelles Thema
trace s.th.	etwas aufspüren, auffinden
trait	Merkmal, Eigenschaft
tranquil	ruhig, gelassen
transitional phrases	Überleitungsvokabular
trigger s.th.	etwas auslösen
turning-point	Wendepunkt
two-pronged reaction	Reaktion auf zwei Ebenen
typify s.th. as	etwas abstempeln als, bezeichnen als
unaffected	unberührt, unbeeinflußt
be unaware of	sich einer Sache nicht bewußt sein
uncivil	schlecht erzogen, unhöflich, grob
unconcerned	unbetroffen
undergo a change	eine Veränderung durchmachen
underscore s.th.	etwas unterstreichen, betonen
undoubtedly	zweifellos
unequivocal	eindeutig, unzweideutig
unity of thought	gedankliche Geschlossenheit
unlimited (point of view)	uneingeschränkter Erzählwinkel
unruly	undiszipliniert, aufsässig
update one's knowledge	sein Wissen auf den Stand bringen
urge that	drängen, daß
utterly	völlig
value	Wert
voice s.th.	zum Ausdruck bringen
weigh the pros and cons	das Für und Wider abwägen
weird	unheimlich, irre
well-equipped with	gut ausgerüstet mit
well suited for one's purpose	gut geeignet für jemandes Zweck
whet one's appetite	jemandem Appetit machen
what puzzles me is	was mir Rätsel aufgibt, ist
with a keen/close eye on	mit einem scharfen Auge
withhold information	Information zurückhalten
a word/sentence is loaded with	ein Wort/Satz ist aufgeladen mit
wretched	erbärmlich, elend